A practical guide to training professionals

Plan, prepare and deliver training like a pro

Edward Chipeta

A practical guide to training professionals

First published in the United States of America in 2008
by Lulu Publishers
www.lulu.com

Design and illustration: **Edward and Tatiana Chipeta**
Editing: **Tatiana Chipeta**
Proofreading: **Tatiana Chipeta**
Layout: **Edward and Tatiana Chipeta**
Cover and back design: **Edward and Tatiana Chipeta**

Copyright © Edward Chipeta 2008

A CIP record for this book is available from the American Library of Congress.

ISBN 978-0-6151-8496-8

This book is published for general information only. Please read Disclaimer for more information.

www.EdwardChipeta.com

About the Author

Edward Chipeta was born in Zimbabwe, Africa. He did his primary schooling in Zimbabwe and went to Malawi for secondary school and University. Ed graduated with a Bachelor of Science degree with majors in Computer Science and Economics and a minor in Financial Accounting.

Ed's first experience with training was during university years from second year to fourth year. He taught Computer Programming evening classes for students that needed extra lessons to cope with their studies. For his professional life, Ed started working as a Management Trainee with National Bank of Malawi and moved to Johannesburg, South Africa, to join Allied Bank as an Information Systems Analyst. While in Johannesburg, Edward taught computer programming and mathematics part-time at Open School, an African National Congress underground school, during the Apartheid era. After a few years, Ed took a Business Analyst position with Norwich Life in Cape Town, South Africa, where he also authored Computer Based Training and ran an employee-mentoring program. Four years later, he secured a job with Nabisco in New Jersey, USA, then Pepsi, in New York, then Las Vegas Valley Water District in Nevada (which is his home), and finally SPL WorldGroup in London, which later became Oracle Global Tax and Utility Business Unit where he works as a Principal Consultant. As part of his expertise, Ed writes technical training materials and conducts client training. His job assignments have seen him travel to London and Belfast in United Kingdom, Dubai and Abu Dhabi in the United Arab Emirates, Karachi in Pakistan, Nicosia in Cyprus, Dublin in the Republic of Ireland, Amsterdam in Holland, Moscow and Perm in Russia, Warsaw in Poland and back again to Johannesburg in South Africa.

Edward continues to work and travel around the world.

You may reach him by email at Edward@AllAmericanGeneralDealers.com.

Dear Reader

Since you are reading this page let me congratulate you for you have just discovered a book that is written with you in mind. I also was a reader just like you picking up books on the shelves and wondering whether I still have to pick up yet another book after this to continue my search.

This is a book for those who would like to start a new career in academic training. You probably know some of the training techniques but would like to know how to conduct yourself professionally. This book touches all the relevant facets of planning, preparing, and executing training the professional way. You will find useful templates and examples of various documents that you will need to create as a trainer. By following the tips and examples in the book, you will be able to formulate your own training program that reflects your style.

The information that I have presented is as exact as I experienced in the years that I have been training and teaching. You do not need to have prior teaching experience. Actually this book is written for those people that have no time to attend a training course on how to be a trainer. This book is meant to be full context handy book such that you may not need another book on this subject.

In conclusion, I would be very interested to learn your personal experience as you take on this journey. Please write to me with comments or questions via email at: Edward@AllAmericanGeneralDealers.com.

Good luck with your new career and I wish you all the best with your endeavors.

Edward Chipeta

Foreword

I am sure you have heard of families in which the members and generations take on the same career. Whether it is in politics, sports, music, military, many other countless professions, you might find that the profession is passed down through generations. We can mention a few examples like Julio Iglesias and Enrique Iglesias in Spanish music, Nat King Cole and Natalie Cole in Jazz music, the Kennedies or the Bushes in American politics, the Ghandis in Indian politics, Muhammad Ali and Laila Ali in American boxing; and Cesare Maldini and Paolo Maldini in Italian soccer. It is easy to think that there may have been explicit influence from one generation to the next or the young generation trying to emulate the older generation, or is it genetic – that the later generation follows the earlier generation without knowing about it? Well, I do not know where I fit in, but all I know is that my father was a teacher for years before I was born. When I was born, he had changed his career and therefore I never saw him teaching. I however remember growing up as a child seeing tons of books on the bookshelf, which my father kept for years. As soon as I could read, I noticed that some of them belonged to his father. I even saw textbooks in my grandfather's handwriting, which appeared to be 'lesson plans'. When I asked, my dad told me that his father (whom I never met) was also a teacher for most of his life. In those days, teaching was one of the most prestigious and respected professions. During my primary school, I saw my uncle teaching Mathematics and he was really passionate about it.

Back in Malawi, in my second year of college I saw the advertisement on the notice board for a student teacher to teach evening classes assisting struggling students. I did not hesitate. All I could think about was the money, of course. However, I felt a sense of excitement when I was going to teach the class. I felt a sense of accomplishment at the end of each class. It felt that it was something I really enjoyed doing. What I did not know is that the Computer Science Faculty Head saw my passion such that he offered me an associate lecture job upon my completion of my fourth year. However, I already had dreams I wanted to achieve. I had long dreamt of finding a way to go to the United States of America. I needed to take on a career that prepared me for that plan. The career that I had in mind was Information Technology (IT) that eventually led me to the US.

After graduation I left Malawi for Johannesburg, South Africa, where I pursued my IT career working as a Systems Analyst at Allied Bank. It was then that I saw the advertisement in the newspaper for a part-time job to teach Mathematics and Computer Programming for high school level. After I was hired, I realized that the school was an African National Congress (ANC) underground school sponsored by Nordic countries. I spent three years on that job. I only left because I was moving to Cape Town to further my IT career. There again, although my primary job was a Business Analyst, I was nominated to draw up and run a mentoring program for new hires from the previously marginalized groups. I was also put in charge of authoring Computer Based Training to train employees on how to use the corporate computer systems.

The only reason I left that job was because I was then ready to get a job in the US. A few years went by without doing anything related to teaching until 2005 when I was asked to perform it again at a corporate level. Even though my real job is a Systems Designer, I find myself performing more training activities than anything else.

I have not been able to tell whether my training passion is genetic, emulation, influence from my forefathers or a deliberate choice. All I know is that I have acquired enough experience over the years and this book is a documentation of that. However I have focused this book on the training of professionals – on-the-job training to assist employees with career growth. I have not included material on teaching learners in a school setting. I feel that this is in the area of teaching, which I distinguish from training. I look at teaching as something that is done in schools. To gain the skills to teach, I see it as something someone has to attend a teaching college for. I see training as something done by someone who has experience in a particular trade and has been asked to share that knowledge with fellow employees. The employees already have varying degrees of knowledge and experience, which need to be grown in a certain direction in such a way that enables the learners to identify and measure the level of knowledge they attained. To me, I see training as an opportunity to learn about the subject that I thought I knew all so well. The questions the learners ask challenge me to dig deeper to know more about the subject. The suggestions from the learners give me a different perspective, which broadens my horizon.

You can therefore be assured that the contents and the techniques in this book are proven and tested to be life-like. Use this book as a starting point for your personal growth in your training career. You will find that training career is 'back and sexy again'!

Acknowledgement

First and foremost, I would like to thank my wife for her encouragement and belief in the things that I do. Her love and support is beyond words. Her suggestions and help editing this book were invaluable. Tons of love, and many thanks, honey.

Secondly, I would like to thank Chris Weatherill, Resource Director of Oracle Corporation, for giving me an opportunity to advance my career as a trainer in such a reputable company.

Dedication

For my wife Tatiana, my best friend, support and peace of mind.

Disclaimer

Information contained in '*A practical guide to training professionals*' *by Edward Chipeta* is for suggestive purposes only. This book contains techniques that I developed for myself. Use this book only as a guide to formulating a style that works for you. I am not making any claim that following this approach guarantees success. This approach will produce varying results for different individuals. This book is not meant for use by students at any academic institution and, as such, statements made in this book should not be cited in answering any examination questions.

Contents

Introduction

This book explains how to conduct professional adult education – mostly 'on the job' training. This is the training of learners that need to know more about their current job activities or the activities they will be required to perform in their next role or learners who need to understand topics about another department that they deal with on an on-going basis in order to understand them and work with them much easier. In most cases, these are learners that have volunteered to come, having been crying for the training. However others come because they have been forced to come in order to improve their current performance.

Since this is education for adults, the learners are likely to be around your age group, both genders, and from different backgrounds. This calls for you as a trainer, to be polite, respectful, and professional. However, because the reasons for attending the training are varied, there will be varied levels of enthusiasm towards learning within and across classes.

As I facilitate a class, I presume that these adults are willing to learn and hence I will not be forcing anyone to learn. Therefore, I maintain my heightened level of energy and passion as I teach and make sure I prevent destruction from those that seem less interested to be in the class.

You will notice that other learners appear disruptive only because they are so smart such that they can see your point before you conclude making it. You, however, have to safeguard yourself from going at the pace of the bright ones. I usually set my pace to be as fast as the slowest person that meets the prerequisite of the training. However the danger of this is that the class becomes too slow and boring for the fast learners and you might not finish what you planned for the course. Therefore I try to strike a balance. As I wait for the slow learners, everyone in the class becomes aware as to who those slow learners are and the slow learners know that they are slow and holding back the class. But consistently, no matter which country I give training in, you would think that these slow learners would ask for help, come early or stay behind after class to practice and catch up. This rarely happens, actually never happens!

Have you got 'it'?

So you want to be a trainer, but do you have what it takes to be a trainer? Do you have the attributes needed for training? Just because you are a subject expert, does that automatically mean you can effectively train?

There is more to training than being equipped with the subject knowledge. Remember that the knowledge that you have makes sense to you because it is your knowledge, you are you, and you have packaged that knowledge in your brain for your use. When it comes to sharing that knowledge and helping people acquire it in a way that it also becomes their knowledge, requires a different skill set and attributes that a subject expert may not necessarily have.

For example, you may have acquired that knowledge in school, on the job experience, or even studying on your own. When it comes to training or educating others, you will be dealing with many factors. You will be dealing with other people other than yourself. You will be dealing with more than one person at a time. You will be dealing with learners with different backgrounds, different background knowledge, different genders, different personalities, and different cultural backgrounds. For this reason, you have to present yourself in a way that each learner (or most learners) can identify with. Therefore you need to dig deep into yourself to exhibit multiple 'personalities'.

Here are some of the characteristics you may need to have or practice on:

- Good listener
- Confident
- Warm and approachable
- Patient
- Cheerful
- Humorous
- Spontaneous
- Logical
- Organized
- Creative
- Assertive
- Empathetic
- Clear and audible voice
- Multi-tasking

- Enthusiastic
- Friendly
- Smiley
- Enjoy presenting
- Excellent communication
- Flexible
- Well spoken (have a creative choice of words, not repeating words, not saying 'uh', 'you know', 'you know what I am saying', 'right', 'like', 'get it?')
- Energetic
- Emotionally sound and strong
- Ready to stay on your feet most of the time

▪ Talk all day

Here are some 'beauty' contest attributes you should have:

▪ Good posture	▪ Smell clean / good
▪ Pleasant look	▪ Clean breath (no alcohol or cigarette breath)
▪ Clean shaved (if you are a man)	
▪ Neat	▪ Well dressed (not 'bling-bling' but well ironed and color-coordinated clothes)

Good trainers are people who are driven and those that pay attention to what they do during training and try hard to improve with each training session. Over the years, I have developed my own tactics such that hardly anyone dozes in my class. I usually get applauses and standing ovation. I also hear excited expression of "Yes!" when a learner really gets it and sees how this is going to change their lives. I am not asking you to fixate on these rewards but that these rewards will come naturally after conducting training regularly and applying these steps that you have acquired from prior training sessions.

Preparing for training

Plan your activities

Once it has been agreed that training is needed and that you are going to give it, you have to start preparing for it. You will need to define what that training is about, what the prerequisite knowledge of the learners should be, and what skills the learners are supposed to acquire by the end of the training. List these as your objectives. With this background, map out what your class should cover to meet these objectives. In turn, map out the class activities to meet each objective. These activities should be choreographed in a way that makes logical sense. For each objective, you should come up with an introduction of that objective. Also explain what tasks will be performed to meet that objective. After that, list the flow of the tasks in a logical manner that will form part of the knowledge transfer. Lastly, formulate your summary or conclusion to refocus the learners' knowledge towards the objective.

If the course covers a lot of material such that you have to divide the training into two parts – first part now and the next part after a break of a number of days, be mindful of the risk. If the second part assumes knowledge taught in the earlier class, you will be surprised that many people will not remember that the topics were previously taught. You will have to make provision for revision before continuing.

Plan your training delivery structure

In addition to choreographing your class activities, also choreograph everything that you are going to do. What your opening remarks will be, what slides you will use and when, what steps you will take, when you will do exercises, what questions to ask the class to measure their learning experience, what you will show, what you will do, and what proof you will show.

All this planning is needed because, in class, you will not have time to think when the pressure is on. Once the training starts, you will be disrupted with questions, you will be pressed for time and you will not have enough free time to gather your thoughts properly and freely. If you do not do this, you might perform the wrong task in the wrong order and will mess up the logical learning process. The result could be waste of time investigating, clarifying and fixing the problems you will have caused. Planning ahead will make you feel relaxed, confident, and prevent panicking as you wonder whether you are really ready for the class. During class, do not be shy to look at your outline and the notes that you prepared for yourself. Learners do not mind because they will know that you did your homework, you are prepared and you are taking this class seriously and professionally. Therefore, the learners know that they will not be confused since you will find your way back on track should you get lost. Besides, even high profile people read from prepared notes. From an actor or actress accepting an Oscar to a leader of a country giving a state of the nation speech. This way you know (barring other reasons) you will cover everything you planned without omitting anything important. However, refrain from reading from your notes. Use your notes as cues or last minute refresher for yourself while presenting from memory. Read them during biological and refreshment breaks (if the learners will not come to ask you more questions). In my case, I make detailed notes because I do not want to re-think something that I already thought about during preparation. I also do not like memorizing stuff, so I write everything down. However, in my detailed notes, I highlight the key points that give me a clue of what that paragraph is about. Only when I have forgotten the details do I take a longer pick at my notes, reading them to myself, and then turning to presenting them to the class from my knowledge of the subject matter. The point to remember when making these notes is to lay them out in an easy to read format so that you can easily find what you need. I usually include page numbers, short headings, and then bullet the notes under that heading. In short, do not be complacent by going to a training session unprepared or without reviewing your notes if you are giving a course similar to the previous one.

Let us recap how I usually prepare for the classes:

- Define what that training is about

- Define prerequisite knowledge

- Define what skills the learners are supposed to acquire by the end of the training and list them as your objectives

- Draw up introductions of each objective

- Map out the material that the class should cover to meet these objectives

- Map out the class activities to cover that material

- Choreograph (create a flow of) the activities in a way that makes logical sense

- Outline the tasks to be performed for your material to meet those objectives

- Attach when you intend covering the topic and how long it will take to cover it

- Formulate how to effectively summarize the lesson to re-enforce knowledge transfer to meet the objectives.

Interview learners and their managers ahead of time

In an ideal situation, it is important that you get the names of learners and names of their supervisors. This is important because it is worthwhile spending time talking to each manager to understand what knowledge they expect the learner to acquire from the training.

You also need to interview the learners to determine their knowledge and skill level and their expectations from the course. (Of course this would be easier if you have physical access to the learners.) This gives you a picture of what you will be dealing with and you can better prepare for it. If the learner possesses less than minimum prerequisite knowledge, you may be able to suggest a different course, or you may suggest what they need to work on before class starts in order to be at an expected entry level.

In addition to getting an insight to the learners' skill sets, you will be able to figure out the learners' personalities. Which learners are extroverts, which ones are introverts? You then have to prepare for both.

Armed with the information, select the right learners for the class - slow learners in their own class and fast learners in their own class. The challenge is in identifying beforehand these types of learners. One way is to talk to the manager and the reasons they are nominating this learner. But sometimes the managers are not that involved in the selection. The learners may nominate themselves. In this case, where possible, you can have a discussion with them about their background and make an assessment of their skill sets. It is not simply a matter of their knowledge about the subject but also the competence levels on how to use the tools they will be using. For example, if you are teaching how to use computer software, does this learner have basic or advanced keyboard, mouse, and operation system skills? In some classes I have taught, some learners were slow but not in the grasping of knowledge but due to poor keyboard skills. They were slow at typing or identifying a widget on the computer.

Also as you categorize your classes as Beginners, Intermediate, and Advanced, are the people enrolling for Beginners really beginners? Some maybe more experienced only attending the Beginners course because they are not sure they know everything that needs to be known at that level. Some may be coming for revision. Therefore make sure that when such learners end up in your class, they do not influence the pace and the direction of the class by their attitudes or the questions they ask. It can happen that they ask questions to bridge their overall knowledge where such questions are advance in nature to the disadvantage of the other learners. By being tempted to answer those questions, you might confuse other learners with less knowledge. In such cases, kindly point out that such topics will be covered in the advanced class. If you feel that not answering the question is interfering with the concentration of the learner, answer the question during the break.

Will the real 'McCoy' please stand up?

As mentioned previously, you ideally need to know the people before giving the course. However, in the real world, you may not have access to the attendees ahead of time. It is more like 'surprise!' on your first day. This means that you have to go round the class asking people to introduce themselves. But first, I introduce myself to give them an idea that it is okay to talk about oneself in more personal terms. In my introduction, I include more of my personal stuff because attendees are always curious about that. Instead of saying the same things over and over to each person that asks me, I decided to create a PowerPoint slide introducing myself. However for the learners, I ask a few items:

- Name

- Where do you come from?

- Why are you taking this course?

- What are your expectations?

- What is your previous exposure to the subject matter?

In my introduction, I show photos of me as a youngster and make fun of them. The learners usually make humorous comments about them. Photos of my college days and my wedding also stimulate humorous comments.

In my slideshow I mention the following:

- An ice-breaking picture of the actor Eddie Murphy, and I claim it is I in my previous life. This is because I have been told I am a look-alike. After displaying that photo, I display my actual photo.

- I mention where I was born and I show a childhood photo of my brother and me and ask if they can guess which one is I.

- I mention where I went for high school. I display a photo of my friends and me and ask if they can pick me out of the group.

- I display a photo of myself and my musical group that I performed with in university for three years and again ask if they can spot me. In the background, the slideshow plays one of the songs that we performed.

- Then I display the photo of my university graduation day.

- After that, I talk about where my professional career started, what I did, and display photos of students, and myself, that I trained as I traveled the world.

- Then I mention that I am married and display the photos of my wedding day. I joke 'sorry ladies, and guys! I am married'.

- I also mention the children that I have and display the photos of them with me.

This usually takes about 15 to 20 minutes. Why do I spend all that time? There are few reasons why I do this.

- It is a good icebreaker. It gets people talking and laughing.

- They get to know me as a person and not as a grade school teacher whom they have to fear.

- Some people tend to identify with me and that rapport usually spills out to outside the class.

- But the most important reason for me is that, this gives me a chance to reduce the pressure and nervousness that I usually feel the first day of class, which most people call 'stage fright'.

- The other important factor is that if people know more about me, they will feel comfortable with me and would learn better and will be able to share their personal experiences that are relevant to the class.

- However, there is one thing I have to safeguard from. I have to make sure I do not sound arrogant, self-centered, and showy. This is because some of my personal and professional experience may sound very impressive to attendees such that they may think that the reason I am telling them is just to boast about it.

Develop your training material

It is usual that you will be asked to give training that has training materials already developed by someone else. That is good, but then go through them and know them really well and deliver them by bringing them to life in your own words instead of reading the materials to the class.

What I usually do is prepare my cue notes drawn from those materials and arrange them in the way that suits my style. I start by listing items in the table of contents. Then I go to item in the manual to pick key phrases that will be cues to how I will be presenting the materials as discussed below.

'Masquerade' – Prepare your trainer notes

Before giving the training, I familiarize myself with the training material. I read them. I practice them. I take the table of contents of the training manuals and paste them in a word processor. I prefer spreadsheet software like Microsoft Excel because I can have columns where I can add notes, comments, data and other attributes like what time I hope to cover that topic and how many minutes it will take me. I use this spreadsheet to number and put in sequence what I will be covering. It becomes easier to re-order the notes. This gives me an indication whether I will be able to cover everything in the syllabus. During the class, I tick off each topic as I finish it. I update them with the actual days it took me to do it. This helps with my planning in the future. That way I will know when I am falling behind schedule or when I am ahead.

In addition to the items from the table of contents, I add other items on the list exactly where they should happen. These include introduction to the topic, exercises, questions, brainstorming, jokes, etc. These items are sequenced exactly the way I need them to be.

All this helps me to be on time, to be organized, to be logical, to perform tasks at the best times that they need to be performed, and plan the exact manner in which I deliver the material. This helps me not to worry that I might forget what I was supposed to do, especially when I have been interrupted by questions or other things. I will know whether or not to start a topic given the time left to a break or end of day.

After planning everything, I step through everything to make sure it flows well. When everything has been checked and fixed, that is when I feel a sense of preparedness. Still, each evening, I step through the activities of the following day to make sure I did not overlook anything and adjust anything that was made necessary by the events of the current day.

'B-Plan' - Prepare for an alternative delivery

If you talk to enough trainers, you will hear that what can go wrong in a class, *will* go wrong. Things that you would normally take for granted will fail. You are going to have a power outage, the projector will malfunction, the air conditioner will not work, the computer server will go down, the room that you thought was booked will be taken by someone else, your computer will not boot, some of the learners will have problems with their computers, your trainer notes which you kept on your laptop will fail to open due to disk corruption, the training material will not be delivered on time, nor will the refreshment, especially the water you need. Need I say more?

You will notice that some, if not most, of the things that will go wrong are out of your control. But is that a good excuse? Maybe. But you and your learners will pay the price when things get back to normal. You will have to work hard to make up for lost time.

It is also reality that training usually starts on a Monday when help may be late in arriving if the decision makers are not in the office yet. Some computer networks may have been brought down for maintenance or for power conservation. Therefore to avoid losing too much time, panicking and starting the course on a wrong foot, arrive at the venue early to have enough time to check things out and be the first one to call for help so that you are the first one to receive service.

It is important to know the contact persons for all the things that are vital to your training. Also, try to learn how to resolve some of the common things that go wrong during training.

Print your copy of training materials. Print your cheat sheet notes. Back up your computer files on an external data media (memory stick, external hard drive, compact disk).

If training relies on software residing on the server, have a stand-alone version installed on you laptop. In this case you will have to know how to setup your computer to act as a server and connect everyone to it. Please refer to Appendix A for an example of how to setup a local server to your laptop.

If you cannot get all the telephone numbers that you may need, at least ask for the organizer's telephone number, or your manager's telephone number, or someone superior who has this training's interest at heart. These would be the people to call when such miss-haps happen.

Even after calling for help, the resolution may take a while. You need to have something to do with the class. If you do not have it, the class will be restless and some learners may wonder off and may only come back long after the problem has been resolved, hence holding back the starting of class. Therefore prepare for an alternative delivery. For example, prepare what you would do if the computer you were relying on no longer works, if the server is down, if most of the learners have to be excused for a certain amount of time. Also have a plan of how to help latecomers catch up.

You could prepare for discussion sessions that prepare the class for the training that was meant to be. This will shorten the time that you will need to catch up when the problem is resolved. Do individual activities, do group activities, facilitate class activities on the whiteboard or flip chart. Do anything, as long as it is relevant to the training.

Rewards

Think of ways to reward your class when they have done well for the day. Reward is something that scientists have long discovered to motivate behavior. We see it being used on animals being trained for a particular skill. We use it with children. 'Eat your vegetables and then I will give you ice cream' or 'if you clean your room, I will give you a cookie'. The same still works with adults. If you promise them what they need or desire after they perform a certain action, then you will see effort towards performing that task. One best way I use this is when I need to catch up with my objectives. I promise them an early dismissal for the day or Friday if we can achieve a particular task by then. Therefore use this to the advantage and not the detriment of the class.

'Oops! I did it again' – What if you make a mistake

As a trainer, you have the most challenging job. You have all those people in the class. Each person has a different personality and different needs and you have to keep the peace and keep everybody stimulated. You are the center of focus for the full eight hours and you are talking most of that time.

With all this pressure, it is inevitable that you might say something that you should not have said, or what you say may be misinterpreted. Also you have to stay neutral so that you are not seen to be favoring some learners. Therefore, when you make a mistake or say something wrong, be quick, ready, and willing to apologize. Make sure you are sincere and do not defend yourself. Understand your mistake, apologize and make a note not to do it again. Be the first to agree that you did a mistake. At the same time, as a trainer try to be humorous about it so that the learners should be comfortable to point out other mistakes you may make in future. However, note that your sense of humor may not fly with everybody since others may think you are trivializing the matter. Therefore vary your humor and remember to avoid stereotype, racial, or sexual humor. I usually joke about myself or about a fictitious third party who cannot be identified stereotypically. Other jokes that you may need to avoid are wife or husband jokes that may be seen as sexist to women or men, respectively.

Planning for training in a 'distant' place

When you are going to give training in a distant place or different country with learners coming from different countries, you have to plan extra things ahead of time for everybody.

Note that some, if not all, attendees may have to fly to this training. Therefore, your timing should allow for no less than 14 days for booking flights. Any less than that might mean the tickets may be expensive.

Allow another 10 business days so that people who need visas to enter that country have enough time to obtain one. This will also enable them to perform any required medical tests. These medical requirements may be for obtaining a visa, or other advisory requirements or personal in nature, and results may take a few days to obtain.

Medical advisory may be required if people are traveling to a malaria region, for example. These people may need to start taking preventative pills two weeks before entering this region. Personal requirement is really for those people that are on chronic medication. They may need to arrange with their doctors and pharmacists to order enough medication to last them for the whole period they will be away. People should be advised not to count on being able to buy this medication in a foreign country. Such medication may not be easily available.

You may need to check travel advisory concerning security risks, mass religious events, political events, or long annual national holidays when many businesses may be closed, flights and hotels overbooked. Things to consider include:

- Am I traveling to a place during their religious pilgrimage?

- Is there a mass workers strike that may affect immunities?

- Is there political unrest or elections taking place that may get out of hand?

- Does your government forbid traveling to certain countries due to political embargo?

- Is there an annual national holiday where most things come to a stop for a number of days?

- Is there a huge trade fair, sporting event or something like that during that time which will make hotel and flight ticket hard to get?

The most important thing, of course, is being able to communicate all this information needed to make arrangements and travel easier and accurate. You will need to be specific and clear about the following items about the training:

- In what country is the training?

- In what city is the training?

- Reference letters for visa application and border crossing.

- Visa needs

- Whether you need to register yourself to the police or immigration authorities after checking into a hotel or whether the hotel will assist in this requirement. This is usually a requirement in Russia and other former Soviet nations. For example, I ran into trouble with authorities as I was trying to board my flight out of Bishkek (in Kyrgyz Republic). I had not registered with the police after entering the country. This resulted in a heavy fine.

- What is the nearest airport?

- Advise on the hotels closest to the venue that are suitable for the attendees.

- How does one travel from the airport to the hotel?

- What is the name of company hosting the training?

- Address of the venue

- Include a local map of how to get to the venue or the office (instead of expecting that with the address, each attendee will get their own map. You owe it to everyone that you make sure that everyone has the exact correct information. This is because even with the address, depending on which map service the attendee uses, the results may be different.). You can ask the attendees to ask their hotel for a taxi service that can be charged to their room. This can save people from having to withdraw lots of cash to pay for a taxi each day and can ensure that they are safe and not overcharged. At the same time, some hotels charge more for their taxi than ordinary taxis.

- Map of the local area for attendees to familiarize themselves with surrounding areas.

- How to travel from the hotels to the training venue?

- Contact person (for security in the building, venue, logistics) for attendees to verify that they have arrived at the correct venue or to call for help getting to the venue or clarifying other details or answer questions.

- How to sign into the building?

- What are security requirements at the venue?

- Will there be someone to meet them?

- Include information about the weather so that people can bring appropriate attire. You may want to advise them to have in their carry-on luggage clothes that suit the weather at destination so that they can change before exiting the airport. For example, include gloves, wool hat, and a coat if the destination has a cold weather.

- Start and end dates of the training and confirm the duration.

- Pre-requisites attendees should meet to attend this training.

You as a trainer may need to find out information from your contact.

- Ask about the venue:

  - How to get to it
  - Whom should you turn to if you need printing done, etc?
  - What are you doing there?

- Logistics:

  - Equipment
  - Network
  - Server
  - Printing material
  - Venue preparation

o   Whiteboard and markers

o   Flipchart and markers

o   Will a language interpreter be needed in class? In the first class I gave in Moscow, I had learners that could hardly understand English and they also had more difficulty expressing themselves both verbally and in writing.

The preceding comments are statements to help minimize chances of undesirable events from happening. You certainly might not be able to eliminate all possible mishaps. Take this as an example. Despite being aware of factors to look out for before planning a foreign training session, during one of my training journeys, I fell prey to the very factors I was trying to avoid. My manager had planned my training trip to Moscow, Russia, weeks ahead. I was told about the dates. It became clear after I had secured a visa to travel there and the training had been confirmed to all attendees and flight tickets were bought that I was to arrive in Moscow on the very day that the Russia presidential elections were being held to elect Dmitry Medvedev after Vladimir Putin's term in office was over in March 2008. I had no idea how busy the city was going to be or how hectic the roads and hotels would be. I planned to slip into my hotel room at 1PM and never to venture out until the following day. But the drama started even before I left home for Moscow. At the local airport, that morning was the first day the new baggage handling company was taking over from the previous company. Also on the weather report on television, there were reports of massive delays to flights in and out of Germany (where I had my connecting flight to Moscow) due to extreme bad weather. That day, I headed to the airport with little hope. The checking in and the boarding went on without a hitch, but we could not take off. The new baggage handling company was struggling to keep up with the workload. This held us back from taking off for more than an hour as we waited for our luggage to be loaded. This delay was endangering my chances of making my connecting flight to

Moscow from Germany. The pilot promised to do his best to make up for lost time. However by the time we arrived in Germany, it was late for my flight departure. But the weather was a double-edged sword that cut both ways. The weather had delayed all flights even the flight I was to take to Moscow. This flight was held up in Moscow on its way to Germany. It arrived almost the same time as my flight. As I sat waiting to board, I watched news on television that showed a near crash on landing of an aeroplane that landed only moments after my flight. This was due to strong winds. Anyway, I made it to Moscow. Lucky enough, the elections were peaceful. There was neither drama nor chaos in the city. I did not even see any evidence of elections.

Remember

On the first day of training, plan to start training late to allow traveling learners time to arrive. Some learners will have problems with flights, and some will have problems locating the venue. You will find that starting at 11AM would be practical. This should allow only enough information for introductions and then break for lunch and start the class promptly after lunch.

Also on the first day, some students will have come straight to class from their flights. Therefore be flexible with your ending time on the first day. People will be tired from the travel. They will also need to locate their hotels, check in, and settle in. It would be considerate to break any time from 4PM but no later than 4:30PM. Keeping learners beyond this time would only make you unpopular.

Another word on giving training in a foreign country is the need to exercise safety in how you go about your moving around in the area. Consider the following:

- Use safe transport like trains and metered taxis.
- Wear a seat belt when riding in a car whether it is a taxi or private car. This is because driving in some countries is rather reckless.

- In some countries, avoid buses and private minibuses.

- Avoid traveling late at night.

- If possible, go out with a local 'guide' who understands the local language and customs.

Other issues to note in a foreign country

- If they talk a different language, learn at least how to say 'Hello', 'Good morning', Good evening', 'Please', 'Excuse me', 'Help please', 'Do you speak English' and 'Thank you' and use them with service people in the restaurant, in the streets when you ask for directions, etc.

- If the learners that were talking in a foreign language now change to English that means they expect you to involve yourself in it.

- If you are going to dine with your learners, always pause before starting to eat or doing anything and observe if there are any customs that are done before doing something. For example, do they wait for everybody to have a plate in front of them before starting to eat? That is to say, if you have been served first before others, do not start eating until everyone has been served. Also after finishing eating, stay seated until everyone has finished eating before excusing yourself and then standing up.

- Notice how people behave and adjust accordingly. Like, do they shake hands every morning when they greet each other?

- What is the interaction between men and women? This is important because the Western culture may not be the accepted way when dealing with people of opposite sex.

'Who is your daddy?' - naming your course

In my experience I have discovered that how you label your classes is as important as giving it. Therefore beware how you name your class. You may be tempted to call the first class in a series of classes, 'Beginners', then 'Intermediate', and then 'Advanced'. The danger of this is that you may run the risk that some people may not sign up for 'Beginners' course because they believe that they have more knowledge than beginners knowledge. But when they show up for the next level class, you realize that they do not even have knowledge that even the Beginners class assumed.

Therefore name your classes differently. You could name them 'Part 1', 'Part 2', etc. or anything that is neutral to the assumption of prior knowledge. You can then go ahead and list the coverage of each class. The learners will have to rely on this coverage to pick their level. In addition, you had an opportunity to interview the learners before your class then you would advise them which class to attend first.

I have had people tell me at the end of the course that they came for this particular class for a refresher since they already knew what the course was about. But they found themselves realizing that there was a lot they did not know and were so grateful that they came for the class they initially judged not to attend.

Creating a course curriculum

s a trainer, it may be left up to you to write the course curriculum. I define a curriculum as a document that lists a set of courses, their contents, and their pre-requisites. The purpose of this is to give the readers an idea of what courses are offered, the contents, and pre-requisite knowledge for attending each one of them. This helps readers to decide whether or not to attend a given course. It may also help the readers to decide which courses they should attend to get the necessary knowledge to attend the other courses. On the next page, I will give one example of such a curriculum. As you will see, writing one is more of an art than a science.

Here is an example template for your curriculum:

	OBJECTIVES The objective of this curriculum is to: - List the set of courses offered - List the contents of each course - List the pre-requisites for each course.
	INTRODUCTION This curriculum is needed to help employees assess at what level of competence they are and how much there still is to be learnt, thereby helping them set learning objectives. The course levels themselves have been structured not by the complexity of each subject in a given area, but by how the subject fits in with the rest of the subjects in the course to form a logical flow of the courses that compliment each other and that properly constitute a distinctive level of achievement. *Etc…*
	BEGINNERS COURSE (Total of … Hours) **Purpose:** The purpose of this course is to… **Pre-requisites:** None.
	Course Topics

	• Introduction to …	
	• How to …	
	Course Topic: Introduction to …	
	This course gives the Learners the skills needed to …	
	Supporting document: Introduction to…	
	Task	**Activities**
	Taking a call from a customer	Answering the phone.
		Greeting the customer.
		Notifying the customer that the call is being recorded.
		Activating a voice recorder.
		Asking the customer the purpose of the call.
	Logging details of the customer call	Place your phone on 'not available' mode.
		Entering details in the computer.
		…
	Course Topic: How to …	
	This course gives the Learners the skills needed to …	
	Supporting document: How to …	
	Task	**Activities**
	…	…

Duration of the course

Careful consideration needs to be given to the coverage and duration of the course. You need to balance the quantity of material to cover in and the total days in which to cover them. These two aspects will determine how much material to cover in one hour. Therefore, plan the material to cover in a given hour. This will determine the pace at which you will run your class. This tells you how much material to cover from break time to the next break time.

Be mindful when you plan to cover a lot of material such that you will require people to attend a 5-day or 10-day course. You might not succeed.

To start with, not many people can put aside 10 days in a roll. Second, you will cover too much that people will not remember much. People will get sick and tired of coming to the class. Hence some people will skip a day or 2 and delay the class when they come back. Others will attend only a fraction of the class. Others will not even book for training saying that they do not have 10 days to spare. In my classes, one or two people always drop out if it is at a client site. In a class of 15, 2 people who booked do not even show up. Another 2-3 will drop out completely. Others will give excuses to come late or leave early.

Common reasons for this are that people are either called back to the desk because there is a crisis in the office, or they have a doctor's appointment. Therefore to prevent this, it is wise to conduct the training at a venue far removed from the site where people work. This way, people will not be tempted to visit their desk to do something quickly. They might not come back if they get carried away with that task.

Having said that, 10-Day class at a neutral venue may have its issues. It might be costly and difficult for people to get to it. The training may have been booked at a rented conference centre at a high price. If it is a venue where people have to travel to and stay in a hotel for the duration of the course, it might be expensive to travel (fly) and stay in hotels.

You might be tempted to shorten the duration, speed up the pace of the class, and keep the class going until late in the day. If you find yourself thinking this way, you are courting danger. Besides the obvious that you will be unpopular, you will burn yourself from exhaustion. You will not have enough time to rest in the evening. You will not have enough time to prepare for the next day, and therefore you will be less prepared and less organized. This will impact the quality of your presentation. Besides, no matter how fast you want to move, some learners will not grasp the material fast enough. Even if they are able to keep up the pace, they will not be able to really appreciate what they are doing to return the knowledge. More important, the brain can only take a certain amount of new material beyond which nothing will sink in. This could leave you and the class frustrated.

If possible, plan a 10-Day class but instead of giving it in 10 straight days, plan more frequent short courses of a day or two. That way you will have more people sign up and attend the whole series of classes. It could be that fewer people will sign up, but you might be able to give repeat classes which people can sign up for if they missed the previous one. They will remember what they learnt because there was no information overload. However this approach works well when giving on-site courses. If people have to fly and stay in a hotel, this would not be the right approach. You would still have to do in 10 days.

The consideration is that you name the course by what the subject matter really is instead of naming it with a blanket name that can be interpreted differently by different people. Make it specialty course. This will ensure that people commit to come and stay for the whole one or two-day course. More people will sign up in total numbers as you give repeat classes so that those who could not make it for an earlier class can have a chance to attend this time around.

Making classes short and small in size makes work easier for you as a trainer. You are not pressed for time and you can relax during break and in the evening (instead of spending the evening preparing for the next day) and between classes.

This arrangement of classes may impact how you plan your classes. When walking the learners through exercises in order to build data needed for follow up exercises, do not assume that every learner is succeeding every step of the way or attended the previous class where such data was built. Also do not assume that they will always tell you when they are behind because they might not and you will only find out later when it is too much to have to catch up with. Therefore, lead the class slowly and walk around to make sure they are still following. You may ask them to tell you what stage they are and what their results are to prove that they are following. These should be things they can only see if they are following. Simply asking if they are still with you is not enough because those that are behind may be too shy to speak up.

'Spring Cleaning' - Preparing the room for training

As a trainer, you are not going to just show up at the training venue as casual as the learners. Once it has been determined that you need to give training, you have to know how many learners will attend and look for a venue that will comfortably accommodate the class. You will need to go and see the venue yourself. If it is physically impossible for you to check the venue, you may want to ask someone close to it to check it for you by supplying a checklist. Check what facilities are in the room. You may consider the few things on this checklist below.

Checklist of some of training room basic needs:

- Are the lights working and bright enough?
- Do you know how to dim or brighten them if needed?
- Are there enough working power points?

- Is there a projector? Does it work? Can you operate it?

- Is the air conditioning unit in working conditions and can you operate it?

- Is the computer network functional if you will need it? Do you know the network guy and the contact details should you need help?

- Is there an emergency exit door or window and can you operate it?

- Is the room easily accessible by people with disabilities?

- Do you know where the toilet facilities are? Do you need a key to access them?

- What about the coffee area? Will coffee and water be provided in the classroom or in a common area outside the class?

- Where do people go for lunch? Is lunch provided as part of the course?

- Note that lack of coffee and lunch could make or break your class. If you expect them to return back early after coffee and lunch break, then consider providing learners with these things to keep them around to quickly return to class.

If these basic needs are met, go ahead and book and confirm the booking. If you are booking this venue electronically, it may be wise to call the person in charge of the venues and confirm that the venue has indeed been confirmed for you and that there will be no conflict with anyone.

You may also need to consider the following:

- Number of learners: Is the number of learners good enough for training. In my experience, a class of about 15 learners is about enough.

- Sitting arrangement: Does the sitting arrangement suit the learning experience your want to set?

- Where is the best place for you to sit / stand? Does the sitting arrangement force you to be in front, or in the middle or at the back of the room? How does that suit your style?

- Supplies: Does the flip chart have enough paper? Is there an erasable whiteboard? Are there pens for both flip chart and whiteboard? Is there an eraser for the whiteboard?

- Size of the training room

- Sitting style of the training room

- Where to sit in the room

- Writing scrap paper for yourself and some learners who will come empty handed with no pen or paper.

- Is the room clean? Will the room be cleaned at the end of each day?

- What about the keys to the room? Will you be keeping them for the duration of the course? Is it safe to leave items in the room overnight?

One thing you can count on is that with all the people in the class, there will be a difference in what the ideal room temperature should be. Some people will want the class warmer while others, cooler. Therefore, again, learn how to set and use the air conditioner. As a trainer, you want your class to be comfortable. What may be comfortable for them may not be comfortable for you. This means you have to prepare to be comfortable whatever the temperature setting. Therefore you will need to dress accordingly. You may need to wear clothes that can be dressed in layers starting with a light top, then a light jersey, then a light jacket, and so forth. That way, when it feels warm, you can shed off the layers of clothes and put them on when it feels cooler.

You just have to accept this fact; anything and everything that can go wrong will go wrong, especially on the first day of training. On one typical day, I found that there was no electric power in the training room, the air conditioner was not working, and the Internet network was not working! Here are suggestions on how to survive these mishaps.

- Know where the main power switches are

- Have an alternative approach to training should anything go wrong

- Have hardcopy manuals

- Have stories

- Have class exercises

- Know the people responsible for servers, computers, and other technical aspects

Printing training materials

Most training sessions require training manuals. If yours is one of them, you need to make sure that the training materials have been developed (written) and ready for printing in good time. If you are using a third party printing company, you have to know that you are not the only one using that service. Therefore request to have training material printed at least two weeks before training starts to allow time for printing and delivery. You will find that the printers will have several excuses why they could not print on time. Prepare an alternative lesson plan without training materials because you will need it more often than not.

If you are traveling or flying to a training venue, it would not make sense to print 15 copies of materials and carry them with you. If you are flying, you might have excess luggage on your flight. It is not just 15 documents. You might need 4 or 5 documents for each learner and then multiply them by 15.

That is a lot of materials. Therefore it is advisable to have them printed locally. Your local contact should facilitate this. You may need to email softcopy documents of the manuals to be printed. You will need to specify the number of copies and format (single-sided or double-sided) to print and what type of covers and binding

It's Show Time! (Welcoming the class)

O n the first day of the training, make sure you arrive early, switch on all the equipment needed for the class, switch on the air conditioner to a comfortable temperature, see that tea and coffee are ready (some learners cannot start a day without coffee – you do not need them to be restless because coffee was not ready).

You have to make it a point that on a daily basis, you arrive at the training venue before anybody. This help to psychologically make the classroom your domain. As learners arrive, they feel better finding you there (it is like a child coming home from school and finding mum home). This way they will know how serious you are about what you do.

If you are traveling to give training, book your flights to get there a day before the training start date – preferably no later than early afternoon. This will give you time to do a dry run of how to get to the training venue by driving or walking so that you do not have to panic looking for the place on the morning of the training. Attendees usually fly in on the day of the training. Do not be like them. On the first day of training you will be able to arrive early to prepare the room and make it your house such that everyone else looks like an invited guest. This will help you calm your nerves if you are like me who usually has a few butterflies in the stomach until I say a few sentences and get the first response from the class.

After you have made sure that everything is in working order, turn attention to yourself to make sure that your personal needs are satisfied. These could be using toilet facilities or performing relaxation exercises or having a cup of coffee. By the time you get back to the classroom and you are about to enter, what do you do? In the meantime, most learners may have arrived in the classroom. You know that the learners will make an impression of you (fairly or unfairly) the moment you step through the door. They will associate you with the last training experience they had. If they had a bad experience, as soon as they see you, some may think 'Oh no! Not another one of those!' Unfortunately there is no other way; you have to fight for your reputation from the word 'go'. Therefore you have to pull your socks up. You have to have your own cheerleading team in your head. As I mentioned, you may need to visit the bathroom and look at yourself first. Make sure you look the way that you intended. Fix your clothes, hair, teeth, and anything else that may be out of place including your posture and facial expression. Is your facial expression saying that you really did not want to be here or is it saying 'this is where I need to be right now'? Make sure your posture is upright and chant inwardly to rev up your outlook. While you are doing all this, anyone you meet around this training facility could be one of the learners in your class, therefore treat them as if they were. You do not need to be embarrassed that the person you brushed off in the corridor or bathroom is one of your learners! Tell yourself: 'This is it! Here we go, it's Show Time!' Step out of the bathroom with your best facial expression, beaming with an underlying smile. Look out for eye contact with people you are meeting in the corridor all the way to the classroom. Nod and smile at them. Step in your classroom and, in your bright voice and friendly tone, say hello to anyone who is there. Approach and shake hands and say 'Welcome'. Again, be mindful of cultural differences when shaking hands, especially if you are a male approaching a female. Make a small talk about something positive. If the weather is great, you could talk about that. If the weather is bad, do not talk about it, talk about something else. Proceed and check that the equipment settings are still correct and your lesson notes are handy. Test out any slide shows you will use. Collect all the markers and eraser that you will use on the whiteboard and flipchart. Review the lighting and learn how to operate everything. If you will be using a computer network, test that it works and make sure you know the technical people to call for help. Test it with one of the learners' computer to make sure it works so that you can give the same instructions to the rest of the class.

On this first day make sure you are dressed in a way that enables you to do any dirty work like crawling under tables, climbing on a chair, etc, but at the same time, looking your best for the first good impression. This is more so because on the first day you are less likely to get volunteering learners to help you.

If you are to give training in a foreign country, do not expect a funfair welcome. You might be given information of where the training will take place and the people at the reception may have information about you. Unfortunately that is where it might end and you are on your own after that. You have to setup the projector, the computer, the sitting arrangement and other things by yourself. You would be wise to make sure that you have your own laptop installed with everything that you need for the training. If manuals were to be printed on site, it would be wise to either print your own copy or at least have it in soft copy on your laptop. In other words, you have to make sure you have your own stuff to make training happen.

To make life easier for yourself, make sure that all the computer files (lesson notes, slides, soft copy of training materials, exercise worksheets, etc) that you will use are copied to a dedicated folder with nothing else in it. You do not need to keep the class waiting while you are looking for the file amongst other files that have nothing to do with this class. In the moment of pressure, it will take you even longer to find the file, if at all. Make sure that the files are named in a very descriptive way. That way the file will be easy to find and you do not want to open the wrong file because some learners will be looking at the projection and watching everything you are doing. If you should find yourself struggling, switch off the projection of your monitor to the projector. However, this may prompt learners to switch off their attention or even leave the room to make a phone call or do something else. You do not want to risk losing their attention. Therefore you have to learn how to use 'extended screen' feature for projecting your computer to the projector. This is a feature that enables you to project one thing while displaying something different on your monitor. That way you can project something 'interesting' (to keep the learner engaged) while you are working on something else. Make sure that your boot up settings allow for extended monitors. Switch on the feature by going to Desktop settings to switch on the two monitors - one for the projector and the other for your laptop. You can find details of how to set up this feature in chapter of how to use a projector.

Once everything is set, straighten yourself up, go wash your hands, and straighten your hair. Come back and stand in front of the class next to your desk. This is where the learners will check to know who is the trainer. Smile, greet, welcome each person as they come in and show them where they can sit. This is because some learners prefer to sit far from the trainer while others prefer sitting closer. Those that sit in front may be doing so because they have poor eyesight or have problems with hearing or because there do not want to miss a thing since they may be distracted at the back. As you stand, your posture should be non-threatening, non-authoritative, but smiley and humble. I know of trainers that like to impose themselves that they are in charge. Guess what, you are in charge whether or not you show it. However, if you show it, you are only making it hard to win the respect of the learners. Learners do not respect you because you are authoritative, but because you are easy to deal with. For me, the most successful classes are those that I excelled the most by being both professional and friendly. Judging from the learners' evaluations, the attributes they described as the best for their learning experience was how organized and prepared I appeared to be, how professional (this is a mouthful word that does not exactly describe behavior), friendly, smiley I was, and a sense of humor that got them through the day. I do not scare to deviate from the class subject when an opportunity to be humorous presents itself. Usually this kind of humor has the most impact because it hits the learners when they least expect it. Sometimes I make fun of what I am doing or what I just said. If what I am explaining ends up being a sequence of complicated logic and I see that the class is getting confused, I abruptly stop and take a jab at what I am saying in a manner that I guess is what most learners are thinking. This usually makes them laugh because they feel they are not idiots for not comprehending what I am saying. I never say 'Yah know what I mean?' It does not help anyone if they missed your point. Uttering this phrase will not suddenly bring sense to something that did not make sense in the first place. Rather, I change my style. I talk slowly, pausing at the end of each sentence to allow them to connect the logic. I may even see if I can graphically represent it. Sometimes I may ask someone to express how he or she understands what I said. Chances are that someone may be more eloquent about it than me. Sometimes it is when one learner is trying to make sense of it that the other learners realize they are not alone in the confusion. As a result of this approach, no one ever dozes in my class and many comment on how fast the time seems to fly by.

The one thing I always do before I start the lesson of the day is to say 'Good morning' even if I said it already to them individually. I do not expect a response and therefore I do not wait for the response or insist that they respond. After lunch, I usually say 'Welcome back'. At the end of the class, I thank the class for attending class and 'being patient during a long day'. Though I do not expect a response to this either, I usually get individual responses 'thank you, for your effort'.

If I give two-week long training, I usually find my energy level fading by Tuesday, Wednesday of the second week. I am not going to promote any use of energy boosters, but sometimes it may be worth using some because you do not want to let the class fade with you. If you feel low, always mention it to the class before they can pick up whether or not you say it. Explain what you think is causing your depressed spirits. You will be surprised how supportive the learners can be. I have had learners offer me energy boosters and other suggestions of keeping fit. Some even escorted me to a pharmacy to pick up some medication. Sometimes the best thing is to make sure that you take it easy in the evenings. Go to bed early and sleep as long as possible. Sometimes you may feel down due to weather changes of a foreign country. Therefore I make sure, I stay healthy and avoid things that may make me sick. For example, I only drink bottled water and also use it to brush my teeth. I avoid open fruits like apples and eat covered fruits like bananas and oranges.

Summary of events of the first day:

- Make sure you arrive early

- Switch on all the equipment needed for the class

- Switch on the air conditioner to a comfortable temperature

- Test the computer network

- Set 'extended screen' feature of your computer to project one thing while displaying something different on your computer

- Arrange the sitting plan

- See to it that tea and coffee are ready

- Use toilet facilities

- Fix your clothes, hair, teeth, and anything else that may be out of place

- Straighten your posture and facial expression

- Perform calming or relaxation exercises

- If you are coffee person, have a cup

- Test slide shows you will use

- Make sure you have markers and eraser that you will use on the whiteboard and flipchart

- Greet and introduce yourself as the learners arrive

- Before the class starts, explain the directions to toilets, emergency exits

- Discuss the class schedule regarding what time to start in the morning, when to break for tea or coffee, when to break for lunch and when to break for the day.

If your class is starting on a Monday, there is a good chance that a few people will arrive late. In fact on every first day of my classes, there is always someone arriving late. Depending on how much crucial information these people will miss should you start without them; you may want to start the training (if you cannot wait) with items that would not matter much if some people miss them. Such items should be such that will not require building on that knowledge for the rest of the day. If you must start, be ready and able to summarize quickly for those people to enable them to catch up. This will eliminate the tendency of these latecomers disrupting the class as they ask the person next to them what they missed. However this summary should be done in a manner that does not encourage people to come late for class next time knowing that you will help them catch up.

As much as we know about learners' arrival on Monday, be aware that learners will plan their flights home for Friday afternoon. Therefore, be sensitive to this and plan to end your classes no later than noon. Local residents also expect ending early. You are not going to expect learners to come back to class after lunch. Be considerate and end your class by about 11:45AM. You will find that learners are even willing to come a little earlier on Friday morning for a chance to leave early.

Moving on, discuss the class hours, rules, and other 'housekeeping' matters that may impede learning. Mobile phones have become a major class disruption. Depending on what group of learners this is, you may or may not ask them to switch off their mobile phones. Your learners may be managers or employees that are responsible for critical activities and have to be reachable, otherwise these people may not have been allowed to attend the class. These people may need to answer the calls. You may ask that they talk quickly since you may have to wait for them to finish the call otherwise, so that they do not miss important class activities. As these learners come back from taking their call, they may disrupt the class as they ask the learners next to them what they missed. This may slow your class down. To keep up with your class objectives for the day, find ways to speed up without losing the class. At the same time be mindful of people that may be in the habit of simply picking up personal calls. This may be because some learners come to class because they were forced by their managers to attend. Such learners will not be motivated and will therefore take any opportunity to skip lessons every chance they get. Some people spend the time receiving and sending text messages. In any case, set an example by switching off your own mobile in full view of everybody. The learners will notice that your mobile phone never rings.

The other major source of disruption is the availability of the Internet in the classroom. Some people will use Instant Messenger software to chat with their friends while you teach. As if the behavior is not disrespectful to you enough, some make it worse by having the sound on such that you can hear the beep (even if it is at low volume), which is very disruptive to you and the rest of the class. Even more annoying is that you can see their faces lightening up as they find the message amusing or frowning, as they are unhappy with the message. Even worse is when they suddenly look up and say 'sorry, I missed what you said, can you please repeat that'. In my classes, it is usually the very same people who are struggling with the lessons who conduct themselves this way and they are the first to complain about the class.

Some people will be surfing the Internet while you teach. But the worse are those that visit video websites like 'YouTube'. As a person watches a funny video, there is no way they can be simultaneously concentrating on what you are saying. This means for the 3 minutes that the video is playing, they have shut you out completely.

So what do you do? Do you ask that Internet be disabled? Maybe, maybe not. You do not need to appear authoritarian. However some corporations may disable Internet in a class as matter of policy. In the absence of such policy, it would be hard to suggest that it be disabled. During one of my classes, I needed the learners to connect to my computer to interact with an application that I was teaching. This required directly connecting to my laptop using an Internet Protocol (IP) address. Unfortunately this connection also blocked access to the Internet. The learners were extremely upset with me even though this is just how the technology works. You just can't win!

'Cutting the tape' – kick-starting training

When it is time to start training on the very first day, you have to draw everyone's attention that now the course officially started. For this, I greet everyone as a class, welcome them, make opening remarks, introduce the course, mention 'house-keeping' items, and then introduce the objectives of the first lesson. This is also another moment when you have to sell yourself to the class because some learners may have formulated their opinion about you by this moment. Therefore show your best friendly attributes - smile, laugh, appear approachable, and non-threatening.

My opening remarks for the training

At the beginning of training, I usually make opening remarks to try to ease learners' nerves, to reach out to them, and to motivate them for the training. Below is a sample of my opening remarks.

'Good morning everyone. Welcome to XXXX (name of the course). The course is going to take two weeks and that is enough to feel me with apprehension if I were in your shoes. I know that the thought of coming for training feels one with anxiety. Having that in mind, I will do my best to make you feel comfortable. As much as we would like to learn, I believe that we can learn more if we can have fun in the process, therefore, I hope you brought your smiles with you and that you will be able to flaunt your sense of humor. You will soon discover that I am not a serious guy. I might even say or do thing you might wonder if that is allowed in a professional setting. The bottom line is we are all humans we need to have fun. Let me also point out the fact that even though I am called 'a trainer' it does not in any way imply that I am more intelligent than you. I am only here to expose this subject to you and facilitate discussions. Some of you may be trainers in your own right. I will therefore not patronize or undermine your intelligence in any way. I welcome your suggestions and appreciate if you contribute any thought processes that you may have. How much we learn will depend on your active participation and sharing of your experience. So, lets have some fun! The toilets can be found … The coffee area is …. Lunch will be … We will have 15 minute breaks at 10AM and again at 3PM. The class ends at 5PM. Any questions or comments?

Introducing the course coverage

Introducing course coverage is very important because most learners will be listening carefully to see if this course is worth their time. You will be surprised how many people come to class trying to convince themselves that they need not be in this class. They will take advantage of any statement you will make that seems to reassure them that they know the subject matter and therefore it would be a waste of time for them to be in this class. I have had people show up for class and leave after 15 minutes saying that they felt that they knew what is to be covered. This behavior is very discouraging and disturbing but do not take it personally. These people are the ones that are going to lose out on the knowledge. At the end of one training day, one student commented to me 'I am glad that I stayed because I have learnt more than I thought I would and I know for a fact that the lady that left knows nothing of what we have covered. She has missed a lot and I will let her know about it'. In most cases, the learner's departure has nothing to do with you. The learner had already decided s/he did not want to be there and was looking for an excuse. However, others may leave because they genuinely thought they already took the class. Others may not leave but will switch off during the class. They will sit there and surf the Internet or work on something different. Therefore for this not to happen, make sure that you introduce the class accurately and clearly. If this course is a level higher than a similar class that the learner attended, clearly spell out how this class differs from the other one. Point out what value it adds. It is best that people leave the class other than stay and disrupt the class.

Delivering the training

In these modern days, many classes being given are usually recycled from previous classes. To simplify the classes, trainers develop PowerPoint presentation documents and use them over and over in such a way that even someone not so familiar with the subject may be tempted to think that s/he could give the class! This usually happens when every fact of the training has been detailed on the slides such that all the trainer has to do is page through the slideshow, reading line by line as they go. This is not training. I would suggest avoiding leading the class through a reading session. A trainer should know the material in and out and personalize them to the class and personalize the material to his or hers individual style. The slide shows should only be developed at a high level and used for summary and should be used to replace interactive learning. I usually use slide show for instructions that I leave displayed while the class performs exercises.

The disadvantage of such detailed slide shows include:

- Takes a long time to develop

- It becomes time consuming accurately updating the material when the lesson content changes

- They are very likely to put learners to sleep

- Take away class interaction

- Leave less time for practices

- Less practice means there is no way of knowing how people will use the knowledge in real life

- Amounts to information overload that little of it will be remembered

- Reduces flexibility in the delivery of training to meet individual group needs

- Increases the chance of the trainer being bored going through the same material every time the training is given

- The trainer misses out on the opportunity to discover something that was not documented hence limits the worth of knowledge to the learners

- Some learners will read ahead of you and will not be listening to you as you expand on what you have read

- May take away the all-important eyes contact with the learners.

However, when developed and used properly, slide shows have the following benefits, to name a few:

- Ensure that the trainer remains organized and logical

- Ensure that the trainer remains on the subject without deviation if doing so would undermine the training

- Ensure that the trainer does not leave out anything planned due to forgetfulness

- Ensure that each training to different groups has the same content – standardizes training

- Enables new trainers get up to speed with the experience of training

- Ensure less need for the trainer to spend too much time preparing for training for the following day

- Forms good documents to learners to use as notes to remember later

- When the diagram is too complex and/or too time consuming to draw in front of the class, slide shows could be desirable.

Some of the guidelines for using slide shows would include:

- Limit the number of facts per page

- Make the statements short

- Use 'large' size font

- Use 'good' line spacing

- Use the statements on the slide as cues for the trainer to elaborate, give further examples, and stimulate class discussion

There are times that I find the use of whiteboard or flipchart better than slideshow. Slideshows that show an already completed diagram without showing how it was built may be too much for some people to take in at once. Some may not know what order to take in the diagram. This is not the case while you present using a whiteboard or flipchart because the learners will follow the logical way that you drew the diagram. They can ask questions at any step of the drawing of the diagram and such questions would be relevant at point in time. When a question is asked on a complete diagram, you may wish the learners could pretend the later part of the diagram were not drawn so that you could explain the question.

Here is a list of some of the attributes for giving a good training:

- Eye contact and appear to be giving individual training to the learner you have engaged eye contact with.

- Spread your eyes around the class by making eye contact with each learner in turns. This way they will feel as though you are paying attention to them individually.

- Vary making factual statement with questions that you ask yourself as a precursor to the next fact you are to say. This may just be the question a learner had in mind.

- On occasion give the learners a chance to answer some of these 'self questions' to measure how they are following the lesson.

- Exercise good time keeping. Learners become restless when you encroach into break time. Some learners hold their biological needs until the break. Others need to make that important phone call. Others are exhausted and need a break. Think about the smokers and the coffee drinkers. Some may have a lunch appointment.

- If the style you planned is not working (as determined by inability of learners to understand or as indicated by learners falling asleep or even indicated by your lack of passion) be flexible enough to change it.

- Tailor and cater to the immediate training needs to suit the challenges the learners meet in real life.

- Encourage learners to share their experience so that you can give examples and exercises suited for them.

- Give humorous examples.

- Encourage questions but do not insist that they ask if they do not take you up on the offer.

- Read learner's body language. Body language can tell you if a learner is lost, has a question, or is trying to communicate with you in sign language to indicate break time, disruption, or a mistake you just did. In most cases, some learners do not want or do not know when to interrupt you for a question. Some are shy to raise a hand or speak up to ask a question.

A point about eye contact

By making contact with each learner, look at their facial expression to see if they are confused or if they are leaning towards the next learner in a confused way or to ask a question. In this case, finish your sentence to the satisfaction of those who were following. As you try to make eye contact, you will notice that some learners will anticipate your eyes and will look away. This could be either they are shy, or they are afraid that eye contact will encourage you to point at them and ask them to give an opinion which they are not ready to do yet. It could be because they are not following the lesson, or that they just do not want to talk. Some learners will maintain eye contact with you because they are in the habit of doing so or they follow the logic better that way. Some could be doing something they should not be doing. They can tell from the volume of your voice that you may be turning your head towards them. In order not to be caught out they will look up and meet your eyes to appear to have been paying attention all the while. As a trainer, eye contact maybe that confidence booster you needed because some learners will nod their heads or do anything facial to say that you have gained their attention.

Also as you make eye contact, even a learner that is following what you are saying may have an associated question on something that your point seems to imply but not saying. That learner may raise her hand halfway as your eyes come her way and then lower the hand as soon she noticed that you noticed her. Make a facial or other signal to her that you noticed and you will be coming to her next because you need to finish your point. As you finish your point another learner may signal you or expressly stop you to ask a question. Make an assessment whether this question neatly completes your point or not. If it does, continue your point making sure you satisfy that question. If the question means giving a new example, say that you will come to that momentarily or mention that it will be covered in the following topics. I usually note it down or even better, I note it somewhere in the whiteboard where it will always be visible (unlike the flip chart where it will be covered when you turn the page). Ask her to remind you if it seems as though you forgot about her. Finish your point and then give the stage to her. Do the same for her, assess if the question is for what you were saying. If so, clarify your point. If it is for a future topic, say so, and mention that it will be covered. Make a mental note or otherwise and remember it when the topic is being covered. Make sure to get feedback from her whether her concern has been addressed. If not, let her ask the question again.

Side discussions

Learners engage in side discussion for a reason – good or bad. These side discussions can be disruptive to the class. Therefore when I see learners engaging in side discussion, I usually stop mid-sentence, say nothing, and look in the direction of the noisemakers. The learners that were listening will be puzzled why I stopped mid-way and will follow where my eyes are looking and they will understand why I stopped talking. Some may take it amongst themselves to hush the noisemakers or the noisemakers may notice the silence and look up to notice that I am waiting for them. Some usually switch to me and explain (without me asking them what is going on) what they were talking about which is usually about the topic at hand. I ask if there is something that they need clarified. Sometimes, I finish making my point and point out one of them to say in their own words what I just said. Usually I do not put my learners on the spot by asking them a question and have them answer in front of everyone. I feel this might be seen as patronizing. Sometimes there is a manager amongst the learners. You would not want to make him look bad in front of his subordinates. However, I ask this question to make them aware that they are not listening and also to know how far back I lost them so that I can start from them. I have to have them catch up because if I continue and they do not know where I am, I will lose them further and they will lose interest and likely cause more disruption. In any case, I let them say what they want to say so that they can get it out to enable them to concentrate from now on. I ask if it is okay for me to carry on.

A point to make about this approach is that I do not look at the noisemakers in a reprimanding way because there may be a valid reason for it. It could be that you made a confusing statement, or it could be that they are talking as to how what you are saying relates to their particular situation, or it could be something silly and mischievous. Therefore some will just wave apologetically and some will do nothing.

The reason I pause is because I know that some learners will miss what I am saying. The talking parties may be making it hard for other learners to hear what you are saying. The talkers are also missing the lesson. Pausing is one way the talker will know that they have been spotted. If the discussion is relevant, they will look at you and say 'we were just discussing how what you are saying is true in our department' or 'I really did not understand what you meant by that' or they might just stop talking and wave you on. You do not need to reprimand them because that will happen by itself as the frequency mounts and other learners start disapproving of their behavior. You also need to give the talkers a chance to get their thoughts out of the way so that they concentrate again. You may choose to ask them to share what they were talking about. You may find that the confusion arose on a point that you made a number of sentences prior to the one that you just finished. Make sure you repeat what the concern is, then step back to the point before the confusion started and start explaining again from there. All the while, maintain eye contact with the learner that asked the question and make sure they are following. You may need to say each sentence very slowly and make an expression on your face asking them to confirm that they are with you so far and proceed when they nod. As soon as you see confusion again at the earliest sentence, stop and re-phrase the sentence. Ask where the confusion is. Draw a diagram or a process or anything to represent what you are saying. Ask the learner what they understand and to what point. If the learner comes from the same background as the other learner in the class, chances are that them too may be confused only they did not show it or they thought they understood and only now they start having doubts. If they have no doubts, ask them to put in their own words how they understand what you said. This is because most people understand a topic, not by the way the tutor explained the point, but how they associated the point to their situation. Now if they come from the same background, they could express how they associated their situation to the confused learner and that could help. At the same time, as the facilitator, take note of the association to understand how these learners learn and from now on make sure you explain your points in that fashion.

Now, when there is continued disruption, what do you do? Do you call their names to alert them that they are being disruptive? Maybe or maybe not depending on the type of relationship you have built with the learners concerned.

Also what do you do when students just leave the class to make a phone call, to use the bathroom, or come back late from break, etc? Do you wait for them or continue with the class? Either way this is a disruptive behavior because when they get back they will ask the learner next to them what they missed. Some will hope you repeat what they missed, or even expect that you will wait for them until they get back.

When a number of learners start talking amongst themselves while you are talking, there is a chance that the learners sitting next to the ones who are talking will not hear what you are saying and the ones that are talking are not even listening to what you are saying. You may also find it difficult to concentrate on what you are delivering when you are competing with people who are talking. Therefore continuing talking is not benefiting anyone. There are reasons why people may start talking amongst themselves. If there are learners from the same team, they may be discussing how what you are saying impacts their team. It may be that they have lost you and they are turning to the next learner for clarification. It could be that they already know the subject matter and do not find the need to listen so they talk amongst themselves. Maybe it is because the topic is something they are not going to use in their team therefore there is no need to listen. Sometimes it is an indication that your presentation is failing to grab their attention.

Whatever the reason, you have to do something. You have to identify the talkers. Have they had a history of distractive behavior? Are they the same people talking all the time? Are they the ones that talk when they are confused about something? Some learners have come to me during the break and said that they could not hear what I was saying because of some people talking. Sometimes you might see other learners straining to hear you. They may even put their palm behind the ear to try to catch as much as possible what you are saying.

The bottom line is that some learners disrupt the class because they already know the subject being discussed and as such find no need to listen. They will talk or walk out of the classroom, use internet, email, send text messages, make phone calls, or come back late from the break. Usually such people may not notice when a topic of their interest comes along. You may find they have problems performing an exercise because they missed a small bit they do not know and did not hear it because they were not paying attention. Find a polite way to mention to them that their behavior may be disruptive to everyone including themselves.

To keep these 'subject matter experts' stimulated, I give them advanced exercises to keep them challenged or I ask them to help the other learners that are having problems.

You need to prepare for learners that want to show that they know more than you and challenge every chance they get. I usually let them talk. Once they are done talking, I validate what they said if it is correct and then give them chances to introduce and give background information to the following topic. This way they get to vent and hopefully that will stop them from disrupting your class. However if the challenge is incorrect, you will need to prove it by showing how it is done – words alone will not work.

However some learners will self-disrupt by openly doing other things while you are busy teaching. They are the ones who would get lost because they were not paying attention. I usually do not waste my time with such learners as long as they are not disturbing other people. I start focusing on those that are listening. In a way, it makes my life easier once I get over the disrespect I am being shown. Usually when they realize that they are being ignored, they start fighting to get that attention back – just like kids really. I do bring them back in though. Most learners behave that way even when they are the ones that asked for the training.

As you mix and match what works for you, you should always bear one thing in mind, do not antagonize anyone. You never know, one day you might have to work with them!

Answering questions

In all situations when a learner asks a question, you may understand the question, but do not assume that everyone has understood it since you may have understood the question because you have a lot of knowledge about the subject matter. It might also be that the question was not asked loud enough for everyone to hear. Therefore, repeat the question and make sure the rest of the class understood the question. You do not want to start answering the question before it is understood by everyone because you will lose those people and they will lose interest and switch off such that they may not notice that you are now back to the topic where you left off.

To make sure that everyone understood the question, re-state the question, and the point where the question arose. Take time to do this. You may have to re-state other previous points. You may have to draw something. You can even ask any other learner to clarify where the issue lies. This way you will know that everyone is on board with the question. The learners may make verbal comments enforcing that they had the same question or that they see why the question arose and that they are interested to know the answer. Others will look up inquisitively, and for others, you may see their eyes widen. By taking this approach, you are also conforming to the learner that asked the question that you understood the question.

However other learners might fake their understanding that you may not know they are lost until they approach you at the break, before class starts, or at the end of the class. But most definitely during exercises, you will see how learners struggle and this will highlight what they missed out or what they did not understand.

When doing 'follow-along' exercises, take one-step, pause, look up to make sure everyone is following. You will have to walk around and check whether or not they are following.

Slow learners

You can mark my word, in every class that you teach there will be learners that are struggling to keep pace with the rest of the class. Even in a class where it seems everyone up to par, there will be someone marginally slower. But I ask you to prepare yourself for a learner that is so slow that you worry for him/her. Therefore as you train from day one, start sizing up learners to see how well they are coping. You will immediately identify the enthusiastic ones and the fast learners. Then there will be learners that you are not sure where they stand. Your initial take would be that they are struggling but when you check their work, you realize that they are keeping up. Then focus your attention to the ones that are 'keeping up appearance'. You find that they make an effort to prove to you that they are following but when you check their work, you notice that it has omissions or they are not doing the exercises at all (they gave up) choosing to follow what you are saying. Lastly there will be those you clearly see from their body language that they are really struggling and as a result are also having problems following the class discussions. These are the ones you should care the most for because they are not benefiting from the class at all.

They are different ways of dealing with such learners. Find a way that works best for you. You may ask them to sit next to you so that you can help them to keep up with the class. But you will notice that slow learners always sit at the back of the class and rarely ask questions preferring to ask the person sitting next to them. This disturbs the person that is being asked and slows the class as you notice that they need help. You will be surprised that such learners will not read or revise at night or before class. They will switch off from class activities as they lag more and more behind. (Note that the rest of the class may switch off if you do not keep them interested.) They may even start entertaining email, surf the Internet and even watch videos on YouTube. It amazes me all the time, no matter what country, the behavior is the same – slow learners rarely ask questions or put any extra effort to keep up. They are the first to leave at the end of the day, usually the last to arrive the next day, and the ones that will play around during break time. These are grown ups, how far do you go to ask them to put in extra effort?

However, to help them, you may ask them to repeat what you said, to see if they are following, instead of asking "Are you with me" because they will say "Yes". Keep checking signs that the topic is difficult for them to follow and look out for signs of fatigue and give them a break.

The other way to make sure they will not switch off is to occasionally call them by name and ask them questions that test whether or not they are following. Ask them for their opinion of what you just said. They may say "I am lost, can you please repeat from …". Make sure you do not lose your patience and do not say anything that suggests the following: "why did you not ask as soon as you got lost?", or "no wonder you got lost, you were not paying attention". There is no need because as you repeat and maintain eye contact, they will listen and ask questions.

To further help, you walk around the class to see how they are doing with their exercises. Also look around the class and note their body language that suggests that they are struggling or they need help.

Smart learners

As much as you would pay attention to the slow learners, you have to equally attend to the smart ones. Not doing so means that you will also lose them. Smart learner need to be kept stimulated and challenged. If they find that you are not doing so, they might lose concentration and start doing other things instead of paying attention. Sometimes they will multitask to feel the unutilized part of their brain. Worse case is that they may start stepping out of the class to make phone calls, stretch legs, kill boredom, or do other stuff because they know that when they come back they will be able to catch up and maybe even surpass those that never left the class. Some may even drop out of the class all together.

You, however, have to safeguard yourself from going at the pace of the bright ones just to keep them interested. I usually set my pace to be as fast as the slowest person that meets the prerequisite of the training. However the danger of this is that the class becomes too slow and boring for these fast learners and you might not even finish what you planned for the course. Therefore I try to strike a balance. As I wait for the slow learners, everyone in the class becomes aware as to who those slow learners are and the slow learners know that they are slow and holding back the class. Since they may be a few of such slow learners, attending to them personally would be time consuming. Therefore I solicit the fast learners to help the slower learners. However you have to be very tactful how you do it. You have to make sure you have the permission of the slow learner to be assisted by the fast learner. The fast learners are always all so eager to help because they feel validated and they get a chance to bring this learner up to speed so that we can move on. This also gives the fast learners something to do and they also learn from the mistakes the slow learners did.

'Say something good' - How to talk (pitch, tone, volume)

A trainer seems to need an endless amount of attributes to be effective. This one is about your voice. I do not know if you have ever recorded your own voice and played it back to yourself. God! It sounds like it is coming from a total stranger. Now imagine that people have to listen to you speak all day…

You cannot change the sound of your voice, but you can spice up what you already have. Talking with an even pitch will surely put people to sleep. So try varying the pitch of your voice in each sentence. As you do that, also vary your volume. To get an idea, turn on any international television news channel and pay attention to how the news anchors talk. They talk loud enough. Their voices have life in them and go up and down in each sentence.

Use subtle learners' body language to gauge how well you are doing. If everyone is alert, talking, laughing and participating, you are doing well. But if you see the learners sliding down their seats, crossing their arms, and yawning, you need to change something fast. Of course this may be a result of other reasons besides your voice. But your voice will certainly get such a response if it is not smiley, up-tempo, varied, and loud enough.

Camp formation

As you go about training from day one, take note of who is hanging out with whom. This is true because as the training goes on, you will see camps or groups developing. Most likely you will see two major camps forming.

There is nothing you can do to stop these camps from forming nor should you be stopping them. The point here is that you take note of them and respond in a way that you can use these camps to enhance the learning experience. For example, if one or two people in a camp are struggling to keep up with the class, you may want to solicit help from some of the people in that camp to help the struggling students. The struggling students would feel comfortable receiving help from people they are already friendly to.

It is equally important to understand why these camps are forming in the first place. Make sure it has nothing to do with you. Some of the reasons these camps form, I have seen them to be racial, 'social class', common origins (nationality, organizational or departmental), and association by how well or not so well they are doing in the class. It is important that you handle the situation in class in such a way as to prevent clashes from developing between these groups in a way that might disrupt your training.

'Trick or Treat'

In an attempt to assess how well the class is learning, do you give the learners a quiz, do you give them an exercise, or do you give them an examination at the end of the training? I personally prefer exercises to quizzes or examinations because the learners learn when performing exercises instead of a quiz or exam which may cause them anxiety and panic which may be a waste of time as it becomes counter productive. It might seem as if you are patronizing them.

Other class dynamics

As you go about training a class, there will be other learners checking everything that you are doing, finding faults and mistakes but saying nothing. Others will be helpful and alert you if you make an accidental mistake. In these situations, do not pretend or fake anything because the learners will see through you. Always acknowledge your mistake and do not be too proud to ask for suggestions or help.

The other thing you will notice is that learners are 'suckers' for interesting stories. Take a look at learners and when they look tired, bring up a story or joke when they least expect it. Tell stories of country you have been to. People like to hear how other people live. But do not tell a story in a way that will make them think that you will be talking about them negatively during your next class with different people.

During the class, use the training session as a source for updating your training material (correcting or enhancing) and learn more knowledge that you can use for the next course. I do so in full view of the class. That way the class feels that they have contributed something to your knowledge. I make it very clear that I am not pretending to know everything about the subject and that I invite anyone with knowledge or different tips to contribute. Every time I give a class, I always learn something new from question or contribution from learners, or from the mistakes that we make in class. I am happy about it because I feel that the class was worth it for me too. Therefore update your training material as you find mistakes. Do not be shy. Learners are happy to see that their contribution is being recognized and included in the training material when they see you update the training material in full view on the projected document.

At what point do you distribute training material to learners. How do you distribute them? If the training is covered in several manuals, do you pile all the manuals at the same time at the beginning of the class or all of them at the end of the class, or do you distribute them as you introduce that subject or after discussing the subject? I would frown upon the extreme case of giving all the manuals at the beginning or at the end of the course. I would prefer the middle ground of giving notes – at the beginning of the subject or at the end of the subject. Each has merits and de-merits. Some students want the manual at the beginning so that they can write notes in the manual. I, however, give them out at the end of the subject because I do not want the learners to focus on the manual but on the class discussion. If there are some exercises that require training materials, it is at that time that I would distribute those manuals. Note that even if you give them manuals, you still have to show them and teach them how to read and use them. Some learners shy away from them and may never read them. During exercises such learners rarely refer to the manual preferring to do try and error. Therefore is it important that you teach them to notice and understand what they see and do and that the manual will only be material to fall back on. See what works best for you.

Plan your course coverage to make sure you can cover everything comfortably. Do not cover too much material because the learner will not remember much. Cover less but thoroughly with practice because practice makes people remember better.

Plan how long you are going to talk. Talking for too long will tie you up and your energy will fall as the day goes by. This fall of energy will be noticed by the learners and will dampen their spirits. Therefore pace yourself. Pause after a few sentences. This also helps learners to digest what you just said and gives them a chance to ask questions. During the pause look admiringly to your presentation, a gesture that will draw their attention to it too. Look invitingly (or inquisitively) to the class. Such silence puts pressure away from you back to the class and it will compel them to say something and anything – a question, a joke, or a personal experience around the subject matter. As this is happening, take a few sips on your water or coffee, think what else you can say to clarify what you just said, think what you omitted, gather your thoughts about what you are going to say and how you are going to continue. This rest is good for you and for the learners so that you should not give too much information to exhaust their brains. Smile, tell a joke, tell a story, tell a related personal experience, talk about a side story that has nothing to do with the subject, just to help everyone relax and take a breather. Since I have traveled the world quite a bit, I tend to talk about my experiences there. People are always curious to know how people live in other parts of the world. I usually show photos and videos that are tasteful and appropriate. Avoid playing music during the break even if it is a low volume. Not all people like music or can work with music in the background. The other reason is that people's taste for music is very varied. You may be tempted to profile your music selection according to the racial and age makeup of the class. In many cases you will not have a homogenous group. You may be right to suggest that middle-aged black people will appreciate Rhythm and Blue music, and that the same age group of whites will appreciate soft rock and modern country. What if some would like classical music, or opera that might be absolutely annoying to others?

Starting and ending the day

On a daily basis, the indicator that you are now starting the class should be greetings. Even though I may have greeted the learners as they were entering the class one by one, when I am ready to begin the class, I stand up and say 'Good morning, are we ready to start?' At the end of the day, I usually say something like 'We have now covered what I planned for us today' or 'From the look of things, I don't think we can finish in the time that is left, therefore we have to stop now'. I continue by saying 'let us recap what we learnt today… any questions or comments?' If there are no questions or comments or after taking a few questions, I dismiss the class by saying 'Thank you for today. I will see you tomorrow. Have a wonderful evening'.

Writing for the class

One of the most important parts of giving a class is knowing what to write for the class to see, when to write it, and how much to write. Remember that you may already be giving them training manuals. The things that you are writing are not replacing those manuals. Only write main facts that emphasize your points.

Whether you are writing on a flip chart, whiteboard, or typing in a word editor while projecting the document, always remember to write in letters big enough to be seen at the back of the class. The best way is to practice writing a phrase which you believe to be big enough and then stepping to the back of the room and see if you can read it and adjusting as needed recognizing that some people may have poor eyesight. In addition to the size of the letter, color also matters. Red and green may not be bright enough to be seen at a distance. Therefore for the most part, use black and blue. Also use fresh markers that do not fade as you write. Always use a clean eraser so that erasing does not leave marks that will make it hard to read anything written on them.

Also when the class arrives, ask to see if they can read your sample text because your eyesight would be different from theirs.

During the training, try not to write and talk at the same time. Do not talk while writing on a flipchart or whiteboard. Your body movements with your back towards the class mean that your voice will not carry very well to everyone in the class. Therefore either talk then write or write then talk, but not doing both at the same time. Also while writing, stand from the side allowing people to see each letter as you write it. After writing, step to the side of what you have just written. Read aloud what you just wrote while pointing at it to emphasize the point and reason why you wrote what you wrote. This will help learners put into context what you wrote and why you wrote it so that they know how to best put it down in their own notes.

Where to position yourself when giving training

Varying the position where you stand when giving training may enhance the learning experience. This is because where you position yourself may be convenient for some but not for others. By changing your position, you balance this out to everyone.

The projector will always be in the same position and so will your laptop. However when not using the laptop or flip chart or whiteboard, walk slowly around the class. Arrange the room so as not walk in front of the projection. Also keep your hands where they can be seen. Do not fold your arms or put them in your pocket, and most of all, do not play with anything in your pocket or in your hand, as it will be disruptive. Stand in one place when taking a question. Walk slowly around the room when answering or asking questions to brainstorm a response. When a learner is asking a question, move away from her and stand at the other end. That way, the learner would have to speak up for you to hear and hence everyone to hear. When a learner shows you something, also show it to the rest of the class by projecting it on the projector or calling learners to congregate around it.

When talking, show that you are interested in everyone in the class. Change position from where you are standing to even out the advantages and disadvantages to the learners. Make eye contact with each learner in turn in a predictable manner to prevent distress to the learner. When making eye contact, for example, start with the first person in the first row and move to the next until you are done with that row, then move to the next. That way the learners know that their turn is coming and if they are not paying attention they know they will soon be 'found out'.

When you walk around the class, do so slowly so that when the learner turn their head and body to face you, they can do so at a slow pace without them knowing that they are following you. Move in such a way that each learner as they turn to 'follow', should not be made to turn 360 degrees. Turn them to about 200 degrees or so, and turn them back to starting point and then turn in the other direction for another say 200 degrees and bring them back again.

Posture: How to stand and give the training

Your posture says a lot about you. It can reflect your work ethic and your attitude. It is best that you adopt a neutral stance. Stand and walk calmly and upright. When you have to walk around the class, do not stress learners by appearing to be too hasty. Walk calmly and confidently in a non-threatening way. Do not appear as though you are walking around to catch people doing what they should not be doing, like playing games on the computer.

Avoid putting hands in the pocket. Rather put them to your sides or behind your back. Empty your pockets off coins, keys, or anything that makes sound. Females may have to reduce the number of metal bangles.

When it comes to pointing at items on a flipchart, whiteboard or projection, stand to the side and point with all fingers and an open hand.

'Show and Tell' – Using a projector

In these modern days, it goes without saying that when you are giving a training, you will need to use a projector for one reason or the other. It could be that you need to project a slide show you created, or you need to type text that you need to be seen by everyone, or you need to show a demo. For whatever reason, you will need a projector.

However a projector is not everything. You can do without it if you have other means of projecting items to the class. These days there are also software programs that can be used to project your screen to the learners' computer screens.

The choice is yours. It is hard to tell which one is cost effective. If you have access to both, the choice will be yours to make regarding which tool you can be more effective with. In both cases you will need to know how to operate them.

If you choose to use a projector, you have to use it in a manner that is not disruptive for the learners. Position your laptop in a way as to minimize having to cross the light path of the projector. Position your whiteboard and flipchart likewise. This means that you need to position your laptop between your projection and the whiteboard (and / or flipchart). This way, when you stand up facing the class with the projector to your right and the whiteboard to your left, you only need to turn you body 180 degrees. You will use your right hand to point at something on the projector and your left hand to point at the whiteboard. This way, you hardly cross the path of the light of the project and you hardly turn your full back to the class.

In this section, however, I would like to discuss about an extended screen feature for your operating system and the projector.

So many times I find myself needing to do something on my computer that I do not need the class to see. It could be because a learner asked a question about something I did not expect and the information can be found in a different document that I need to look at. Sometimes, while the class is performing an exercise, I may want to prepare something for the next segment without projecting it on the projector. I could switch off the projector one way or the other. But this may not be practical because the class may be working with items projected. Sometimes switching off the projector can be disruptive to the learners who may think it is time to take a break. In these cases, I use the operating system extended screen feature. This also prevents you from accidentally displaying something private. If you are doing something that is taking a while, you can project something 'interesting' (to keep the learner engaged) while you are working on something else. See Appendix B for how to setup your projector for extended screen.

'Looks can kill' - Your mood

We have heard of expressions like 'behavior breeds behavior'. While giving training, you will need to watch your mood because mood is contagious. When you are gloomy, it will be reflected in your body language and presentation and that will be passed on to the class. As you are busy facilitating a class, some learners will be checking out your personality and your other behavioral traits. One day, a learner approached me during tea break. She said: "I am glad to see that you have warmed up because when you walked in this morning I thought you were moody and I knew something was wrong with you." I know for a fact that I was in my usual pleasant mood and nothing was bothering me. I just responded that "I love training and this is why my mood has improved now that I am training". I did not want to appear to be full of excuses that might seem like I took offence with what she said. From that day on, I made sure that when I was in an area where the learners may be, I peck up my mood even when nothing is wrong. If the learners are already in class, I pause before walking in and practice my smile, brighten up my face and walk into the class like that. I greet everybody and make a comment that gives an impression that I have a positive outlook of the day.

The learners will also pick up on how you talk and the phrases and words that you tend to use frequently. This can be a disruption to learning. Therefore being aware of this will help you vary your tone, your vocal pattern, and your words. You can also tell what the students have picked up on if you pay attention to their behavior. For example, I did not know that I used the word 'Yap' (for 'Yes') too often until I heard a student repeat it each time I said it. That was a hint that I used it too much. Now I use it less – at least I think I do - because I catch myself just before I say it and use a different word instead.

'He said, she said' - Use of pronouns

These are the days of political correctness — so people say. Despite increased liberties afforded to people, people still find themselves not saying exactly what they would otherwise have said because they have to be politically correct. Unfortunately as a trainer you have to abide by that rule because in your class you will have people from all walks of life with varied opinions who will easily get offended if you are not politically correct.

Without sensitizing the issue too much I will cite this example… When giving examples, if you are a male, are you using and making reference to things that are more sports in nature? If you are a female, are you using baby or shopping examples? What I am saying is pay attention to the pronouns you use and how you use them. Each gender tends to use pronouns that mirrors their own. When you pick up a book in a bookshop and read it, you may be able to tell the gender of the writer by noting how often a particular gender pronoun is used.

In my examples, I make an effort to use female pronouns 60% of the time so that the female learners can note that. I will say, "A supervisor has a decision to make. She may decide that…" and use a male pronoun to make reference to the subordinate of that supervisor. If you say it in the reversed gender: "A supervisor has a decision to make. He may decide that…" females will notice what they may see as a stereotyping that females cannot be bosses.

One afternoon after making an effort to use female pronouns all morning, I used male pronouns and one female learner asked: "Why does it have to be a HE, and why not a SHE?" My effort paid off because one of the females quickly came to my defense such that I did not need to defend myself: "Just this morning he was giving female examples" she defended me.

Therefore make an effort. If you are a male, listen to the radio, watch television, read a newspaper or a 'female' magazine, note something significant about a mall nearby and pick up something feminine and positive to mention as an example or a story in such a way that it reflects that you are in tune, in touch and are interested in matters that affect women without sounding patronizing.

If you are a female, this could be an easier task to do. Just switch on television on a weekend or look at the back of a newspaper. You are likely to find a lot of sports. Pick various sports activities. Depending on what country you are in, the majority of men that love a particular sport will vary and this may also vary by race and age. If you are in the USA, you may want to notice basketball and (American) football, if the majority of the learners are black since majority of white males will love it too. If the majority is white, you may want to mention baseball and golf and probably some tennis and motor racing.

If you are anywhere in the world and you have majority West Indies or Asian (Pakistan, Bangladesh, Sri Lanka) men, try cricket. If you are in France,

UK, Argentina, Australia, New Zealand, and South Africa you cannot go wrong with rugby and cricket.

For the rest of the world (Africa, South America, Asia) including UK, Germany, Italy, Spain, Portugal and others you cannot go wrong with soccer (football).

A successful trainer will give positive examples that creatively mix race and gender. I must emphasize that the comments should always be positive. If you must give a negative example, use yourself and your friend of the same gender and race.

If you are female, you may have noticed that I have made stereotype statements about females and males. This is the reason why I am mentioning it to you, the reader, so that you should not make this mistake.

Questions

One of the essential parts of training is measuring your effectiveness and whether or not the class in reasoning with you. One way is to ask short questions in between your presentation. When I ask a question I usually do not give an answer right away. I walk the learners through a thought process by asking a set of questions, answers of which are geared to help them think over the nature of the question and start thinking about answering it. Sometimes, as the facilitator, you yourself may not know the answer to the question and you may want to tap from the many brains in the classroom that have varied experience. This way you get an answer from the learners contributing bits of information they know.

The other use of questions is to get the class to learn how to quiz themselves in order to resolve a challenge they may face. Get the answers and ask a follow up question and steer them towards the answer or towards something that resembles an answer, if you yourself already know what the answer is. However if you are faced with a real issue or question that you do not know the answer to, note it down and promise to research for the answer or find someone that can answer it. Do keep your promise.

The other approach I take in answering a question is not answering it myself but proving the answer by 'showing and telling'. For example, if you are teaching learners on how to use a machine or computer software, a question maybe "what happens when…." Or " How do I ….". Instead of giving a verbal answer, I usually say "Don't take my word for it, lets go and find out…" and proceed to step through the steps towards the question. I use this approach for a couple of reasons. First, it is possible that I may have misunderstood the question I hence give a wrong answer. Second, the answer may seem to be a collection of words that the learner has to remember and regurgitate when asked by someone later. Such a response is not helpful since it cannot be used in practical situations. Third, when you step through a process and show how to derive an answer, the learners do not have to memorize the answer (or doubt the answer) because they saw for themselves what happened and therefore can confidently perform it when put in that situation. Forth, in stepping through the response, new questions may come up that help with the learning experience and expand the topic coverage. Firth, simply answering the question makes the learners passive 'riders' on a joy ride and they might get too comfortable and doze off.

A point to note is to avoid asking leading questions that may be answered by a nod of a head or "Yes". Questions to avoid include:

- "Do you agree?"

- "Are you with me?"

- "Ok?"

- "Understand?"

- "Good so far?"

- "Shall I move on?"

- "Yah know what I am saying?"

Practice asking questions one way and then re-phrase them if no one is making an attempt to answer. Be guided by their body language to see if you need to ask again in yet another way or give them more time to think about it.

It is one thing to ask a question, it is another to take a response. Observe if the learners are over answering the question. This could be due to the learner showing off or not knowing the answer and hoping that one of the statements they are making could be correct.

There could also be more than one learner that would like to answer the question and some may be disappointed if they are not given the chance to answer it. For some this may be the only question they can answer or would like to re-phase the answer to have an opportunity to determine how well their understanding measures up to the correct answer. It could be that they do not completely agree with the answer given earlier. You also need to give all learners a chance to talk. This way they know they are going to answer all the questions asked since they will be asked to answer the question in their own words. However in this approach guard against a learner saying 'I have the same answer as the one just said'. You would have to ask that learner to re-phase what was said or why they agree with the earlier answer.

Without judgment, take any answers as they come whether the learners give correct or wrong answers. The learner with the right answer will be so passionate that that learner will state why the other responses were not correct so that you do not have to say it yourself because you do not need to kill the learners' confidence by letting them know that their answer was not correct.

Dealing with difference of opinion with learners

As a trainer, you have to maintain peace with all the learners in the class. You should make sure you do not appear as though you are favoring some learners over others. Therefore as you present, do so with an open mind and humility just in case you say something wrong; you will need their empathy. You also want to be able to gracefully redeem yourself from any oversight on your side. Since you spend the whole day talking, it is inevitable that you might say something wrong due to various facts. As you talk and as you are center of attention and always engaged, you may lose the ability to look at things from a different perspective and hence lose you trend of thought or even omit to mention something important.

As engaged as you will be, should you find yourself challenged by one of the learners about a point you are making, your first assumption should be that you are the one who has got it wrong. Take a moment to reflect and ask for opinion from others or better yet, ask the challenger to walk everybody through his thought process and point out where you went wrong.

Regional differences

If you travel the world to give training you have to be aware of regional and cultural differences. Even though you will be interacting with people in the business world, their culture will still filter into the workplace. The best way is to do some research to read up on the business and ordinary culture of the people in those countries before you get there.

In addition to being culturally aware, you also need to be politically aware. You need to know the politics to judge what precautions you should take for your own personal safety. In the classroom, it is always advisable to never bring up politics. It goes without saying that when in the Arab world, you are not going to mention words like terrorism, Islam or Israel, for example. Never chat up women or maintain eye contact more than enough to acknowledge her presence and definitely no handshaking or sidelining a man in a conversation in a manner that may be seen as a preference to a female. Therefore, as you give examples in a class, they should be relevant with regards to local heroes, avoiding politics and racial talk.

However these regional differences could prove even more difficult when conducting brainstorming exercises with subject matter experts. The two main problems I had when I worked in a Muslim country was that, the women sat at the back of the auditorium and as a result participated less than men. Noticing this, I made an effort to involve them. However they spoke in a low voice and they sat far. It was hard to hear what they were saying. As a result, the men repeated their sentences or completed the sentences for them. It turned out that the women sat at the back because that is where they 'belonged' – not to mix with men. Also they could only speak when talked to or explicitly prompted. This meant that they could talk when I prompted them. If I did not prompt them and they had a comment to make, I would have never known about it and hence the comment would have never been voiced. Therefore I made sure that prompting them consistently did not sound as though I preferred them to men.

The most challenging aspect about dealing with these women was the fact that their heads were covered completely (including the eyes). They all wore black and most were built physically in the same way. They did not sit in the same order when they came back from a break. This made it difficult when I had to follow up on a comment made before the break. It was hard to associate names with the person. I had to try to memorize the sound of their voices and their mannerisms with not much success. It was embarrassing to ask their names again and again. It was even worse when they asked me to their offices to collect supporting materials.

In the 'West' (UK, Holland, Cyprus, the US) and even Africa, I behave exactly the opposite. I make sure to chat up women and maintain eye contact more than enough to acknowledge her presence. My eye contact should be long enough to acknowledge her as both a person and an intellectual and professional. I make sure I am ready to shake her hand when she presents it and shake it firmly enough to not appear to treat her as a 'weaker' sex. I should be ready to note what she said and take an opportunity to amplify to the group that I took the idea and suggestion from a female. I can do this with a sense of comfort that the male counterparts will not be that offended. In making these statements, I am not pretending or acting. As a matter of fact, I genuinely respect and value women.

When in South Africa, when I give examples, I make sure that the examples mention black and white (Afrikaner, if possible) equally.

As you go to a foreign country, pick up a few polite words and use them when you get there. You will be amazed how the locals warm up to someone who is trying to learn their language. Ask to be taught a few more words and make an attempt to use them with them. But be aware what words the learners teach you. For example, while giving a class in Pakistan, my go-to-person was a female. She and her friend taught me good words. Each morning I would sit with them to learn a 'word for the day' in Urdu. But in Cyprus, the class taught me a few Greek words to use in class to bring the class to attention when they start talking to each other. Each time I used them they would laugh. I thought they laughed because I sounded cute. It was only when I boasted to a colleague who is a Greek speaker that I learnt I had been taught very inappropriate and unprofessional words – those were swear words!

Learners behavior

Dealing with learners is almost like dealing with your children at home. Each of them is different, with different needs and demands. Therefore you will find that some learners will be very friendly to you and some will not. Some will want to hang out with you during breaks and some will avoid you at all cost: 'don't mix with the teacher' mentality. Some, it is because they are concerned you might talk about the training during the break when they are trying to get away from it all.

Some will pay attention and some will not. Some will be restless and some will be anxious. Some will be quick with exercises and some not. Some will try to move ahead of the class by anticipating where you are going and some will try to move fast to be one step ahead so that if they make mistakes, they can fix them before others catch up. This could be that they are scared to be labeled the slow ones.

Some learners may have an annoying sense of humor that they project throughout the course of the class. The worse part is that the learner does not know about it and yet the rest of the class is annoyed by it. Not only can it be annoying, but also can be distractive to the learning process. It can be very trying to you as a trainer because that learner expects you to appreciate his sense of humor and respond to it positively when you know that you cannot. So you have to respond in a way that does not hurt the learner but at the same time in a way that does not encourage the learner to do more.

Always pay attention to their behavior. When the learners start talking amongst themselves, there is always a reason. It could be that they are no longer following the class but are shy to speak up. They could have become restless due to lack of positive stimulation from the subject that you are discussing. Respond accordingly. Find out if they are lost and revise starting from where they got lost, or give them a short break, or tell a stimulating story, or change your approach to the subject you are discussing.

Some learners may be too busy to attend your classes. They may come to the class on condition that they can pick up their calls and / or multi-task. Therefore you might find that they may be typing up an email or a report or even developing a PowerPoint presentation. Since they are absent minded, they will miss a few things and may ask you to repeat what you said or ask a question you already answered for someone. Maintain your calmness and answer the question without making a nasty remark like "We already discussed that a few minutes ago, were you not listening?". You should appreciate that these people would not have attended the class at all. The problem, however, is that these are the very people that may say that the training did not do much to improve their job performance, without consideration of the fact that it is because they were not fully committed.

The learners will also note the words you use. Try to check yourself and the words you use. Listen to what they say. Sometimes when you speak they may repeat the word you said which is an indication that you use it too much. Vary the way you talk so that it is not monotonous to the learners.

Mind your language

As a trainer you will be on constant scrutiny from the learners. Do not ever think that what you say or do will go unnoticed. Your personality, your mood, your words, your promises, everything will be under scrutiny. Therefore do not think you can fool all learners by falsifying something or pretending that your 'experiment' succeeded.

During one course, I made introductory remarks and set out objectives for the course as usual. The course coverage looked as though there was not enough material to fit in the time available. I mentioned that if there is time, I would include other topics. However reality was that I could not finish the 'little' that I had planned due to technical problems (power outage, computer server being down, more questions asked than I expected, and generally that things took longer than I planned).

After the course was done, I went around switching off computers and came across one computer where the learner had left the MS Word document open. When I read it, it contained quotes about statements that I had made and which ones I had delivered on and which ones I did not. It also included what we had covered for each topic and how we went about doing so. Besides these being notes, they were also an account of assessment of to what extent I had kept my word. Therefore be careful what you promise. Make sure you deliver on it. If you cannot deliver on your promises, mention that you will not be able to do so and why. Do not pretend that the learners will not notice if you keep quiet about it.

Also beware that some of the learners may also be professional trainers that are looking to learn some techniques from you. One trainer confessed to me that he picked up some tips on how to run a training course. I felt both flattered and vindicated.

Case studies: 'Trainer-learner' – when training a trainer

As you go on in your training career you will one day come across a learner who is currently a trainer or was a trainer. Depending on the character of that individual, this could be very challenging. The question is how do you handle that situation when it arises? Here are a few cases that I experienced.

Case Study A:

The case involves a trainer that was attending my class because she was not sure she knew everything her job required since she had never been trained even though she had trained workers in her department with the knowledge she acquired over the years. As I give training I encourage people with real life experience to make some opening remarks. I do this to measure how much they know already and also give them a chance to be heard since people with knowledge usually desire that. She made her remarks and it was time for me to continue. However, as I proceeded with the training, she kept interjecting as often as she could and sometimes completing the sentences for me. When it came to practical work, she rushed ahead of the class since I wait for everybody to be on the same pace so I can talk and give more information every step of the way. I have a reason and purpose for setting up the particular practice scenario depending on what else that we will be doing later. This means those that forge ahead risk taking a different path than the rest of the class. By the time I realize this, their project is ruined and they can no longer effectively participate without going back and re-doing everything. This happened throughout the course. In some cases, she would take the approach that worked but was either longer or shorter but had risks. This meant she never learnt anything new since she was doing things the same 'old' way.

What was most disappointing was how she would interrupt me openly and strongly disagree with me before even seeing the end result. Sometimes she would just shake her head in disapproval. I would let her talk and asked what the other learners thought. Most would have no opinion since everything was new to them. Instead of fighting with her, I would suggest that we take her approach and see what results we got, and then I would ask her to let the class try the approach I was suggesting. In most cases, she would say 'Oh, I didn't know you could also do that…. That seems easier and quicker… I still prefer my approach, though'. For the class, I encouraged them to see for themselves the Pros and Cons for each approach.

Case Study B:

In this case, even though she had not attended my classes despite signing up for them, she and I worked together because she had the information management wanted shared with the rest of the team. But because she is only specialized in one area, she could not train the class that was going to cover material outside the boundaries of her knowledge. That is where I came in. She would say, 'So you will be giving training…? I like training and I don't take nonsense from anyone in my class. I keep a tight grasp on the class. If I catch anyone dozing, I order him/her to stand up in the aisle until he/she is awake. I sometimes bring someone with me to class to watch out for anyone sleeping or not paying attention. Once I catch them, they are in trouble. If anyone is disrupting the class, I call them aside during the break and threaten them that I don't appreciate their behavior. If they continue, I kick them out of my class and report them to their manager. As I train, I just surprise them with questions. I just say, You! What is …, or how do you… If they fail to answer they are in trouble. I report them to their manager that they are not paying attention'. That is how some trainers train. I wonder if anyone would like to be in this class. Oh, maybe that is why she did not attend my class fearing that I could be like her…

Case Study C:

While giving training at another client's site, there was a lot of politicking going on. The individual that wanted to be a trainer was sidestepped for me. However she was asked to be in the class as a student. Instead of being a learner in the class when the training started, she started behaving as an observer of both the learners and the trainer. She did not hesitate to undermine me when she had a differing view. I was lucky that some learners were vocal and expressed that they felt that she was making my job difficult instead of letting me go on with what I had planned. A few days in the training, this individual walked into the classroom and announced 'Exam time! Put everything aside. You have 30 minutes for this test and the results will be revealed to your managers'. I had no advance knowledge of this. I pulled her aside and asked her about it and she replied 'I just came up with the idea now. We have to be on top of these students. We have to push them to learn'. I was an external consultant and therefore I stepped aside and watched her torment the students…

Case Study D:

In this other case, I was not aware that I had a trainer 'in the house'. He had prior experience and I noticed that in some place he was coping and in other he struggled. It is only at the end of the course that he asked to say something. 'I don't mean to sugar coat anything because I have not been forced to speak. The fact is that I am a trainer and I have learnt a lot. Not only have I learnt the subject matter, I have also picked up a few training techniques, and therefore I am very happy to have attended this training.'

Case Study E:

This situation started on the very first day of the training. It was a very small class with two learners. There was no projector and I was told by the training sponsor that the training is supposed to be supported using a Third-Party software to project my screen onto the learners screens in place of the traditional projector. The sponsor showed me how to operate it.

When the class started I started projecting my lessons as you would with a traditional projector. Within an hour of doing this, LearnerX vehemently started objecting to its use. She demanded that she have uninterrupted control and access to her computer. She argued that she did not want to be trained that way. She did not want anyone pointing at things while introducing the topics. She said she prefers that I stand in front and describe in words what they should be seeing on their screens. This was a challenge for me because I had no way of knowing whether they were looking at what I wanted them to see. It also meant that I had to talk more when describing where to find something when it would be easier and accurate to point at it. The other issue is that she was so vocal that she undermined the interest of the other student as she said 'I believe I speak for her as well when I say....'

Anyway, I changed and stopped using the software. This meant I had to walk around the class and stay on my feet all the time to make sure they were following and looking where I wanted them to. This meant I could not be at my computer to perform the activities that I was leading them to.

The following day, a new learner joined us. In bringing up to speed, I took this opportunity to summarize what we covered the first day. As feared, there were problems with the exercises the learners were working on and I could not tell what was causing it since I was not doing the exercises with them as I had to walk around not being able to show them on the projector due to LearnerX's objection to the use of the projection software. In trying to isolate the problem I spent my time in class troubleshooting the problem. As I did this, LearnerX became restless and started making sarcastic comments suggesting that I had led them the wrong path. She was reluctant to work with the class to find the problem. I eventually asked for help from Technical Support team who discovered that there was a technical problem from their side that was causing our problems. This was to be expected because the training was being performed in a Test Environment where things were being changed and tested. I tried to steer back the class on track by trying to explain what we were doing and how we should proceed. LearnerX stood up and said 'I think I have heard just about enough, I am out of here'. She left. I continued with the class for another hour summarizing what we were doing, and how much of the objectives of the day we had met. I answered all the questions the learners had and clarified everything they wanted clarified and LearnerX missed all that.

On the third day, LearnerX was hardly participating in the class activities. She spent her time in class playing Solitaire and opening and closing documents. Before long, the exercises for the other student looked more advanced than hers. Then she complained 'Why is my exercise looking different from the other students?' I was surprised at this question from someone that was not doing class exercises and still expected her work to look just like those actively participating. I simply mentioned that it was because she was not doing the exercises.

Throughout the morning, on occasions that LearnerX listened in, she would make comments undermining the comprehension of the other learners and challenging my statements. I had to go to unnecessary length to justify my statements. She would also make sarcastic comments to the other students like 'Its very simple honey, why can't you see that!' or 'Dream on! This could never happen in real life.' or 'Why do we have to do the activities that are done by various departments since it's making us go round and round?' When other learners ask questions, she would jump in to tell them the wrong answer. I had to go length to undo what she said. As I did that, she stood up and said 'I am going outside, I will be back when you are done explaining to them'. The most worrying thing was that her intimidating behavior was making it difficult for the class to speak up. One learner only spoke when LearnerX left the class.

During lunch, LearnerX stayed in class and went out just as everyone else was getting back in. When it was time to start, she was not back. I had to continue with the class. By the time she came back, we were planning how to best utilize the last training day, the following day. I gave her a chance to express her thoughts about it but she said 'If anyone asks me, I have not learnt a damn thing all these past days! We keep jumping from one thing to the other. One moment we are functioning as an employee of one department and the other we are performing activities of another department, and so on. Why can't we just learn how to operate the buttons that we see in the system? Instead of the business processing, we should be spending time learning the buttons of the system.' I responded by saying that learning buttons is part of the curriculum but since this class is only for 3 short days instead of the standard 10 days (The days started at 9:30AM because LearnerX said she was not a morning person and we ended at 3PM because I had another class starting at that time), I felt it would be more beneficial if we covered topics that would be difficult to study by themselves. But LearnerX kept fighting for another 15 minutes claiming that she was speaking for everybody in class. In the meantime, the other students were making eye contact with me and gesturing that she was wasting our time. I asked what the rest of learners felt and they said they would benefit more by learning the business processes that is what they would be expected to do. One learner said it would not be justifiable that we spent three days only learning how to click buttons.

I looked at the clock and we had just an hour to the end of the day. I knew that she would continue to disrupt the class if I did not give her what she wanted. I asked if it was okay with the class if we covered a topic on clicking buttons for that last hour of the day. They did not mind. LearnerX was excited but the other two were bored to death. I could not even finish in an hour as LearnerX asked lots of questions and at times I had to explain things over and over while other learners sat yawning with arms crossed.

Throughout the class, LearnerX kept saying 'When I train, I do this...' or 'I think training should be done by....'

Even though LearnerX was that difficult, I still felt that she was capable of following the class as well as the others. I think her personality was getting in the way.

Conclusion

By looking at these cases, one gets an impression that the wrong people are in the wrong field. Some trainers should not be trainers but the sad part is that they themselves do not realize that. It is no wonder many learners only go to training when they have been forced by management. They are afraid of this kind of bullying behavior from aggressive trainers. I know that there are many good trainers out there but the few scary ones have traumatized many would-be learners. This may explain why when a trainer has a kinder and gentler approach, the learners can immediately feel the difference. Some learners have approached me during the break and said 'I don't know how you do it, but I could not be as patient as you in the face of this trying crowd'.

I have had trainers in my classes before. Despite reservation they may have had about my training style, they were sensitive enough not to disturb those who seemed to be benefiting from my style. None have been as destructive to the learning process as LearnerX. Her behavior made it difficult for me to bring out the best of me to train in a manner that would be beneficial to everyone.

Training is an honorable profession. We owe it to ourselves to behave humanly as trainers so that the learners can get on with the business of learning.

'Self love' - Taking care of your needs as a trainer

The success of a training session depends firstly on the disposition of the trainer and how well prepared he is. Therefore it is important that as a trainer, you take care of yourself. You know yourself and what you need to get the most out of you. As a basic necessity, make sure you have water to drink during class. Have your personal hygiene tissues handy to blow your nose or clean your glasses and hands. Have your emergency headache medicine handy. You may also want to have a spare comb in your bag. If you are a female trainer, do not forget your makeup kit.

As a trainer, you will find out that it is hard to find time for yourself in the 8-hour day. From the moment that you arrive in the class, you are hard at work. You may find that there are learners waiting with questions. You start answering and find that it is not going as fast as you thought it would. The problem is not with you. The learners may be slow at understanding or they may want to be given the whole solution instead of getting a hint and doing the rest of the thinking themselves. Some bring their real life question on the subject matter. They expect you to provide a solution for them that they can immediately and directly apply. They are not interested in the guideline as to how to go about it.

In one class, one student kept disrupting the class with the questions that she said were burning business issues that her manager was expecting her to solve later that day. She said her manager said 'Now that you are on training you ought to know the solutions'. Not only does this disrupt the class by making you digressing, it also robs you of the ability to stick with the structure and plan for your class.

As expected, when you schedule the class, you should make sure that you give the learners frequent breaks for tea, lunch, and biological needs. That should not be just for them. What about you? You need this maybe more than they do. You need time to reorganize your thoughts. You need to make sure you are on track. You can only do that if you have the time to disengage and reflect for a moment. You need to rest your voice, you need to drink water, you need to rest you legs by sitting down, you need to make a phone call, check business email, remove yourself from the gaze from the learner, and a chance to scratch yourself! The list goes on. The better you take care of yourself the better for the learners, because you will stay a fresh, sharp, organized and energetic trainer. The learners themselves have plenty of time to disengage. They can disengage when one learner asks a question that they already know the answer to. They can close their eyes for a minute or two and think of something different. You, as a trainer, do not have a chance to think of anything else since you are talking every minute. If you dare to think of something different, you might accidentally say it out loud as a slip of a tongue.

You will notice that as soon as you announce a break and you take one step towards the door to go visit the bathroom, one learner stops you for a quick question that leads to another. Before you know it, you have been occupied half the time of the break. Once that learner is satisfied or realizes that the break is almost over, he lets you go, but guess what? The other learners who already had their rest have come back to catch you quickly before the class starts. You start answering the questions until you find that the break is over and you did not rest, use bathroom, and sip coffee.

You could do a few things to make sure you also get your rest. Announce break while you yourself are closest to the door. Leave as soon as you announce it. Even when someone tries to stop you, say you will be right back. If you find yourself having too many questions to answer, let them know that you feel this is a perfect question that would benefit the rest of the class and suggest that you answer it when class resumes. If the question is very personal, you could suggest answering it at the end of the class. This way you get your rest. I know many learners do not like staying long after class. When end of class comes, dismiss the class and ask those with questions to remain behind. You will find that the questions will be straight to the point and they will not hold you back unnecessarily because they need to rush home.

During lunch, when you sit with the learners, you may find that some learners are not able to talk to you about anything different from the course subject matter. They ask you about the course and you have to talk while eating. Your brain has to keep thinking. Because you are talking between eating, you find you take longer to finish lunch and use up the time that you could have used for yourself before the class starts again. However other learners ask course related questions because that is the only conversation they can come up with you. Maybe you need to start a conversation about something different, something that will make them do the talking. Of course, you could choose to sit at a different table.

Sometimes at the end of the class you will find that there is usually one guy that stays behind to ask you questions? Ironically, it is the ones that are struggling with the material that escape through the door as soon as you announce that they can leave. The guy that stays behind is one of the hard working ones that are really benefiting from the training. Therefore you do not want to refuse to answer his question. So you do. He will keep you until it is convenient for him to leave, leaving you with no time to yourself. You find that it is late. You have no time to prepare for tomorrow. What do you do? You take work home and work from home to be ready for the class the next day. You could use the same line – this is a perfect question to benefit the rest of the class, let us leave it for tomorrow.

Of course, it is not only the learners asking question that will take away you rest time, you may also find that because you had no chance to disengage, you ended up messing up your trend of thought. You will find yourself using the break time to bring your thoughts together before the class resumes.

All these things deny you the chance to rest and relax to return with a fresh perspective. You become very exhausted and worn out because you are fully engaged and you sustain this for the full 8 hours. Think of a car. Imagine driving with your foot constantly on the gas pedal without occasional relaxation. Not only will you get a clump in your foot, you will also use up too much gas and your car may heat up.

Find out what kind of questions the learners are asking you. Do the questions reflect that they were not listening or could these questions have been answered in class at the time that you were discussing the subject. Were they shy to ask in class for fear of appearing dumb, or were they simply absent minded? You may defer such a question until the class resumes if it is related to the course objective. Tell the learner that you feel the rest of the class would benefit from the question and you would prefer spreading the response to everyone.

You need to take care of yourself. Take your time during training. Do not rush. You are the boss. Stop and take a sip of water. The learners themselves are eating, chewing, sucking, and drinking, why can't you? The learners walk out of class any time they feel pressed for bathroom, why can't you do the same.

For your sanity, you may want to grab your lunch, you tea and sit somewhere isolated and get away from it all. It might seem anti-social but you need to remove yourself from it all. How often do you hear parents saying "we need to get away from the kids". It is not that they do not love their kids, but they just need to disengage in order to rest and recover from the demands from the kids. That way when they come back they are more energetic and psychologically sound and more desiring to be with their kids because they missed them. View the learners the same way.

Trainers want you to appear to be accessible, patient, understanding and giving. Guess what? All these are enough to drive you nuts or leave you extremely exhausted. Therefore, do not treat yourself this way. Do not let this make you hate your job. Do not let anyone spoil your free time after the class because in the end everyone is going to lose. A worn out trainer means a less effective trainer and the whole class will suffer.

One way to prevent this from happening is to make sure that days before the course starts, you prepare your material, plan your delivery, your examples, and every little thing so that you will not need to worry about it when training starts. That way you will be able to maximize your rest every little chance you get. The other benefit of this advance preparation is that you will not need to stay up late in the night preparing for the following day. You will only need to stay up to fine tune your existing plans. Should you need to prepare, you have to do that at a solitary place so that you are not disturbed. This will enable you to finish your preparations quickly to afford yourself rest. You may want to get your personal stuff organized and ready to leave at the earliest opportunity. As soon as you dismiss the class, you should be ready to pick up your stuff and leave so you are not held back.

If your training is in a form of a 'getaway session' where you may be housed in the same hotel as the learners, try not to get sucked in with what the learners are doing because when all that is done, you may still have things to prepare for the next day – something they do not have to do. You might end up going to bed very late.

The other way to take a break is to prepare exercises for the learners to perform individually. Sure some will come and ask you questions, but by and large you will rest. As other learners complete the exercise, ask them to assist the other learners so you will not have to do it yourself. That will boost the confidence of the fast ones. You get your rest. You get a chance to prepare for the next segment.

Also be mindful of the questions that you are being asked so that they should not use up your time unnecessarily. You might be asked about something not related to the current course. But because you are the trainer, they kind of expect you to have unlimited knowledge and answer those other questions even when they do not directly relate to the current course objective.

Take this for an example. One particular day, I arrived 30 minutes before class. I decided to setup data for the course in the software that each student was to use for their follow-along session. The previous day had indicated to me that if I were to let the students do this by themselves, they would mess that data up before it was even ready for the lesson of the day. When it was time to start the class, I was still working on it 5 minutes into the class time. When the data was ready to hand over to the students for the follow-along, some learners still lagged behind. Some even messed it up such that I still had to go and help them fix it. The data got messed up even though they had instructional manuals in front of them and we were reading them together! As a result, when it was time for break, I had to use the break time to help those struggling learners. After going round helping everyone, each person had a chance to go out and have tea or coffee with scones and biscuits. There were scones and biscuits enough for everyone to have seconds, but by the time I needed to go for a break, when it was time up, there was nothing left for me. The learners had sat there and ate everything and no one thought about the trainer. The same with the bottle water. Some learners had even taken two bottles for themselves without counting how many bottles were there and the number of people in the class. There I was, no tea or biscuits, now no water. How inconsiderate!

When lunch came, I tried to get to the eating area soon enough to avoid the same mistake. I made it just in time because I was held up by my boss who had called me knowing that I was now on break. I dished my lunch from the buffet setting. As soon as I sat down, one of the managers in charge of re-engineering, joined me and said "can I ask you a question?" The one question ended up taking the whole lunch. The lunch is usually 30 minutes but she kept me for 1 hour. Then I had to go back to class. For the afternoon break, there were questions flying. I barely had time to grab a drink. When the class broke for the day, students waited for my availability to answer their questions. By the time I completed answering the questions, it was time to go home but I still had not checked email. As I arrived home, one of the managers called me on the phone and kept me for about 30 minutes. When all was done, it had been 9 hours that I was on the spotlight. I still needed to have dinner and prepare for the class for the following day.

Here is something to consider. When giving training, do you stand throughout or do you sit down on occasion. You need to take care of yourself by balancing standing and sitting down. Also make sure that you wear comfortable shoes that will not hurt your feet should you stand for long periods of time.

As you see, your job as a trainer can be very demanding.

Appearance and hygiene

L ets face it, during training you are the one thing that the learners will be looking at all day long. It goes without saying that the learners would rather be looking at something presentable. I am not saying that an attribute of a trainer is to be good looking. I am saying, look presentable enough to look at and smell clean enough to be close to. You will be standing in front of people and you might be bending over some learners to see what they are doing to help them. This means that your breath should smell fresh too.

Days leading up to the training check your wardrobe and plan what you will be wearing. Usually during training the learners dress down to casual. However as a trainer, this is a normal day at the office, therefore dress business smart, whatever that means in your environment. If you are a soccer fan you must have noticed that most team managers dress in a business suit including a necktie despite being a sporting event. For the managers, they are at the office and so are you.

For men consider dress shoes, dress pants and a dress shirt. Tie could be optional. Visit a barbershop and ask for a clean-cut hairstyle and shave your beard. Forget the professor bearded look we see in movies because we are talking about your career here. Wear cologne that is not too strong since you might be coming very close to the learners and sometimes leaning over them while showing them something on the computer or the training manual. The clothes should be properly ironed and tucked in. You can fold your sleeves once since you are working. As for colors, try colors that are not too bright. Try black, grey, and soft blue. Choose black for shoes. Make sure they are comfortable to stand and walk in.

Female trainers should aim to dress in a manner that does not invite unintended sexual attention from men. Also avoid dressing in a 'masculine' way. Avoid shirts, low-cut tops and low-ride pants revealing the mid-rim abdominal skin. Try black feminine looking dress pants. Your top should either be a tuck-in one or should at least be long enough to go lower than your pants' belt. Loose cotton tops are better since they hung in place all the time unlike tight non-cotton top that usually lift up as you reach up to write on a whiteboard. You do not need to spend the day pulling down your top to cover the exposed skin. Wear a subtle perfume. In short, avoid looking too sexy and looking too masculine – aim somewhere in between. Also lose the 'library lady' look but do pin your side hair (with a clip or something) so that you do not have to brush it off your face all the time or throw your hair behind with a swift move of your head. I bet some men would replay that in their minds in slow motion!

Make sure you take a shower every morning before going to class. Avoid smoking during the day and smoke when class is over. Avoid drinking heavily in the evening in such a way as to have an alcohol breath the next day.

Here is a summary of what we have discussed.

- Look presentable

- Wear clean clothes without rips

- Dress business smart (dress shoes, dress pants and a dress shirt)

- Choose comfortable shoes to stand in

- Choose black, grey, and soft blue colors

- Men iron and tucked in that shirt

- Women leave that mini-skirt home but remain feminine but cover the mid-rim

- Take a shower

- Smell clean

- Brush your teeth and cut that cigarette

- Maintain a fresh breath, cut that alcohol

- Shave off that beard

- Comb your hair

'Who is zooming who' - Course Evaluation

Evaluation is one of the tools that can be used to measure the current training and improve the future ones. Not only does it assist in improving efficiency and effectiveness of training, it also improves training content and methods, quality of training materials, venues and other aspects of training. Therefore this is a very important aspect of training.

Focusing on the trainers, evaluation identifies areas that the trainers need to improve in their training skills by getting suggestions from learners. The learners view is very important because how the learners receive the knowledge is a measure of the trainer's effectiveness. The trainer has to cater to the learners and therefore what they think about how well you did is relevant.

These reasons for evaluation should be borne in mind to prevent abusing this purpose. Evaluations could easily be used to rebuke or reprimand trainers or learners. It is therefore very important to remind evaluators that they are immune from 'persecution' for the statements made on the evaluation. Therefore the people reading these evaluations should bear this in mind to make sure that the evaluators did not abuse this immunity by making false statements.

What should be on the course evaluation?

Now what should be included in the evaluation? Just about anything that we need to know about the training, would be my initial response. However, do not get carried away. My advice is to include enough questions to represent a sufficient assessment of the training in a manner that would not skew the results. The questions should enable a judgment to be made that is balanced and fair. Too few questions may give a wrong impression of how good or bad the training was. Too many questions may be hard to interpret and make readers come to a wrong conclusion. Too many questions may exhaust the evaluator in such a way that the last questions might not be responded to with similar energy as the first questions as they rush through them. Therefore maintain a balance.

Here is a sample evaluation form. You can pick and choose from the list.

Course Evaluation

Please spare a few minutes to complete this course evaluation form. Information provided in this evaluation will be used solely to improve the learning process.

Course Name:

Date: _____

Location: _____

Trainer: _____

Your name: *(Optional)* _____

Please rate the trainer for these attributes from 1 to 5 (1 being poor and 5 being outstanding):

1. The trainer provided atmosphere in which to ask questions.

Poor ○   ○   ○   ○   ○   Outstanding
     1   2   3   4   5
Explain: _____
_____

2. The trainer effectively interacted with learners.

Poor ○   ○   ○   ○   ○   Outstanding
     1   2   3   4   5
Explain: _____
_____

3. The trainer created a non-threatening learning environment.

Poor ◌ ◌ ◌ ◌ ◌ Outstanding
　　　1　2　3　4　5
Explain: _____
_____

4. The trainer met course objectives.

Poor ◌ ◌ ◌ ◌ ◌ Outstanding
　　　1　2　3　4　5
Explain: _____
_____

5. The trainer trained in line with course materials.

Poor ◌ ◌ ◌ ◌ ◌ Outstanding
　　　1　2　3　4　5
Explain: _____
_____

6. The trainer related training to real life situations.

Poor ◌ ◌ ◌ ◌ ◌ Outstanding
　　　1　2　3　4　5
Explain: _____
_____

7. The trainer was professional.

Poor ◌ ◌ ◌ ◌ ◌ Outstanding
　　　1　2　3　4　5
Explain: _____
_____

8. The trainer made the training enjoyable.

Poor ◌ ◌ ◌ ◌ ◌ Outstanding
　　　1　2　3　4　5
Explain: _____
_____

9. The trainer was friendly.

Poor ○ ○ ○ ○ ○ Outstanding

    1   2   3   4   5

Explain: _____

_____

10. The trainer was knowledgeable.

Poor ○ ○ ○ ○ ○ Outstanding

    1   2   3   4   5

Explain: _____

_____

11. The trainer presented the material in a logical manner.

Poor ○ ○ ○ ○ ○ Outstanding

    1   2   3   4   5

Explain: _____

_____

Please comment on the following:

Your professional background regarding this training

I include this to help interpret the rest of the comments.

_____

Training duration

_____

Frequency and length of breaks

_____

Food

_____

Training venue

Training materials

What aspects did you like about the training?

What improvements can be done to the training?

Overall course relevance to you

Comment about this evaluation form

Other general comments

'The hard way or the easy way?' - Method of collecting evaluations

When asking for evaluation, you need to decide what form you would like to ask for it. You probably have two choices - the paper way or the electronic way.

Paper method

The most traditional way is to compose an evaluation like we did in the previous section, print it on paper, and hand it to the learners. The evaluators fill out the paper form and hand it in.

There are many issues with this method, a couple of which are:

- You have to print the forms. Usually training is done at a removed location and the printer may not be easily accessible. Of course, you could have had these printed at the same time as when you were printing the training materials.

- The learners have to fill in by hand. Great! What if they make a mistake or they run out of space? You have to print another one? Do they have to rewrite the rest? Will you have a printer this time? The common mistake is in the rating of 1 to 5. Which digit is which? Is 1 outstanding since it is number 1 or it is poor because it is a low mark? Learners usually make this mistake because they come from different backgrounds.

- Handing in the paper work is a game of 'cat and mouse'. Some learners want to remain anonymous. They will complete the form and wait for the rest of the class to finish. They will collect the forms and randomize them so that the trainer does not know which form is from whom. Others prefer to put the completed form into unmarked envelopes.

- The drama is done, now to whom will they hand over the forms and how. Most people prefer that the forms be handed over directly to your manager even though they know that you are going to read them anyway.

- Sometimes more than one manager may be interested in the evaluation of this training, how do you distribute these forms to all of them if they all need to see them 'immediately'?

- It does not end there. Say you had a class of 20 learners, how do you summarize all that information in a timely manner in order to make sense of what the learners are saying collectively?

Advantages

Learners feel that the forms would be authentic since they are in their own handwriting.

Electronic method

These days most big corporations use electronic method to accept evaluations. These can be done anonymously and submitted directly to the manager of the training department that formats them for management consumption. A copy of the report is then sent to the trainer.

Advantages

- No printing needed

- Mistakes can be corrected by the learner

- Submission is quick

- Formatting is easy

Disadvantage

- Learners may not feel that these evaluations might not be compromised.

- The computer / server may crush before the evaluations can be submitted. You need to have an application that allows learners to save their evaluations before submitting.

- If there is a bug in the software, the results will be distorted and / or hard to interpret.

- Developing / buying the software may be prohibitively expensive.

'Timing is everything' – When should you ask for evaluations?

The time when to ask the learners to fill out the evaluation form is very important. Since I value these evaluations so much, I would like to know that the learners had enough time to express themselves. Usually learners fill out these forms at the end of the training. But I feel that is not the best time to do that. The reason is that learners will rush through these evaluations because they need to leave. Therefore, I ask them to complete the evaluation as a first thing in the morning of the last day. If a learner has not formulated their impression about you and the training by that time, there is little chance that they will in the remaining few hours. This strategy has helped me get lengthy, detailed, balanced, and perhaps objective evaluations since people are not rushing anyway. But you have to make sure not to read the evaluation until after the training is over.

'Crunching the numbers' - Writing an evaluation report for the class

Evaluations are very important to your career growth as a trainer. Trainers that are new to the game may worry as to what the learner may say in the evaluation and may be tempted not to ask the learners to fill one out. I used to feel that way but these days I look forward to evaluations. I am interested to hear what the learners think. I think my experience as a trainer and the confidence in my ability make me feel confident that I may still have done a good job. However, I do not let that over-confidence go to my head. That is why I still ask for evaluations. I need to know whether or not I am improving as a trainer. I need to know what I should do differently next time. This helps me with my planning.

The other reason I do not worry about what the evaluation will reveal is because I have been there before and I feel I can take any criticism without feeling like my world has collapsed. I must admit, though, that it is never pleasant to hear something negative, but in the real world, you know that there is always room for improvement.

In most cases, it is left to the learners to evaluate the course as well as the trainer. As important as this is, it is equally important for the trainer to write a class evaluation for management. If management is not interested, write one for yourself anyway and link it up with the learners' evaluation about you and the course. The reason is that the learners will make statements that seem true from their point of view but may not be aware of (or might omit to mention) the other dynamics that you as a trainer see when standing in front, what you had planned, and other issues.

For example, it is very common to get a comment that says that the class was very slow. Learners that are smarter and quicker than others usually make these comments. You may be lucky if the learners that were holding up the class would say, "the class was too fast". Actually, if the slow learners do not say that, then I did my job because the pace must have been comfortable for the slower learners such that I did not leave anyone behind even though I may have annoyed the fast learners. You only frustrated one group that felt the class was very slow but not both groups, including the slow group, felt the class was very fast. It is better if others felt that it was slow (than if they were to say it was too fast) because there is a good chance nobody was left behind and hence they learnt what they were supposed to. Hopefully the irritatingly slow pace did not make them switch off and miss out on learning.

In such a case, your report would say that you identified that there were other learners that needed extra help to complete their work or needed more explanation to understand the topic. These comments may help in future when selecting learners to put in the same class. You will have learnt from these experiences.

Even though the evaluation is about you and the course, it could also be about the evaluators themselves. If everyone specified their names and one did not, you can tell who it is. If that person gave a negative evaluation, there may be a motive for not giving their name. This means you have to read this evaluation carefully and put everything into perspective.

'The moment of truth' - Reading the evaluations

Different people have different opinion as to how the evaluations should be handled after the learners have submitted them. Some prefer making them absolutely confidential and suggest putting them in a sealed envelope to be opened only by the trainer's manager. Others know that trainers need to know how they conducted the training. Such learners only want to be anonymous during handing in the evaluations and hope that no one else put their names on theirs in such a way that it becomes easier for the trainer to know who filled out the one form that did not have a name on it.

I have no objection with the evaluation going to my manager. I actually prefer it. But I know that managers are usually very busy and may not get to them in a timely manner while at the same time, I need the feedback quickly while the memory of the class events is still fresh so that I can appropriately identify areas needing improvement. Therefore, I collect the evaluations, read them, make copies for myself and forward the originals to my manager. If you are lucky that your manager trusts you that way, do not do anything to damage that trust by manipulating or forging the evaluation, whether possible or not. Doing so also defeats the purpose of evaluations.

Now reading the evaluations… It is literally a case of 'good news and bad news'. That is the whole idea – to learn from the bad news and to consolidate on the good news.

Yes, the bad news is hard to swallow, but I'd rather read that than have one-word responses like 'Yes', 'No', 'Okay', and sometimes no comment at all. That does not help me know where I stand and where I should be going.

At the same time, good news is thrilling to hear. It boosts your ego and you feel that you on the right path. It boosts your confidence for the next time you give training. The reason most people are afraid of public speaking (which training is and more) is the fear of making a fool of themselves in public. To make matters worse, with training not only do you have to do public speaking, you also have to be logical and factually accurate.

My experience and positive feedback from the past training means I am more confident. However that does not mean I am overconfident and complacent towards training. I still rush back to my hotel room after every class and stay up late in my room preparing for the next class. Even though I know what I need to train, I still want to plan what to deliver and how to deliver it. I want to know that what I planned will work as planned. I do not like surprises while standing in front of a class. That explanation 'You know it works, I don't know why it is not working now…' does not go down well with learners. For that reason, I choreograph everything, even sometimes my 'jokes'. All this goes towards helping me feeling more confident. When my confidence is apparent to the learners and it makes them feel that they are in good hands. A well-planned delivery means that you will create less confusion in the minds of the class and therefore increase the learning experience. Most comments I have received on my evaluation are:

- 'He is a real professional'

- 'He is very organized'

- 'He appeared to be very prepared'

- 'He is very logical'

- 'He is easy to understand'

- 'The best trainer I have ever had'

- 'Many trainers should learn from him on how to give a course'

- 'Were you trained to do this?'

- 'He loves his job and it shows'

These comments are remarkable, especially that I did not pay them to say these remarks! Therefore when comments like these are made, I feel vindicated. I feel that all those late nights were worthwhile.

However staying up late preparing for class does not guarantee good performance or good evaluation at the end of the course. But still you cannot simply walk into a training room and expect to deliver the best training ever if you did not prepare. What I safeguard is that, having put in all that effort and the evaluation comes out poor, it should not feel like all that effort was a waste of time. If I planned my classes as always but still get poor evaluations, it will be easy to identify what part of my planning needs twigging to improve the training. If you have no plan and no style, you have nothing to go back to and fix.

Make sure you state on the evaluations form that their names are optional – they do not have to give their names. For the most part, it is not important who said what as long as they were objective. However sometimes when the evaluation is in sharp contrast to the rest, it may be important to know who the evaluator was in order to understand why the evaluation came out that way. This is because if you were poor in your delivery, all evaluations should generally say the same thing. If you were average, some will rank you higher and others lower. If you were really good, the evaluation will also reflect something like that.

After reading the evaluations I give them to my manager. It is important that he sees the poor reports so that when the good reports start coming he can notice my improvement. Sometimes your manager might be an experienced trainer who can help you grow. It is also easier to celebrate your successes with your manager if you are able to discuss the poor reports as well. Therefore, nothing is really lost when you get a poor report if you really want to improve.

There is another point to make. There will be learners who will dislike you the first moment they see you. This could be motivated by any number of things. The learners who are likely to act this way are those that did not come to training out of their free will. This could be misplaced resentment. The ones that came because they really want to learn something will have an open mind. I remember one day giving training where I was the third trainer in 4 weeks of training the learners had been having. After introducing myself, this learner asked me something. However he had an accent very difficult for me to understand. English is not my first language but I have traveled to many countries and mingled with many people of all walks of life such that I usually do not have a problem with accents but this one was really difficult for me. Therefore when he spoke, I thought I understood him and responded to him but the look on his face told me that my response was not right. I asked 'did I misunderstand you?' 'Yes'. 'I am sorry, please help me understand you'. His response, "Never mind!' and he turned away and withdrew from class participation for the following minutes. I knew I had to reach out to him but it was clear that he was angrier with me than he was disappointed with me. I needed to make sure he cooled down before I could talk to him. However, he made a recovery by himself and started participating in class. Still my gut feeling told me that he had not forgiven me. For once, I did not know how to handle the situation with him. During that day I could see that he had a friend in the class. His friend, although he was participating, was overshadowing other learners. Each time I put an exercise on the board for each learner to participate, he would be the first one to stand up but would do the whole exercise and rob the other learners of a chance to try. But of course some of his responses were not correct and we had to correct them during revision. It so happened that he had previous experience and he wanted to show it off but seemed not happy to have gotten other responses wrong and he would not admit it until presented with proof. The two of them had held senior positions in their prior jobs in previous companies.

Throughout the training, I noticed that the two of them disrupted the class by talking to each other and each time I tried to find out what they were talking about, it was about something different. When it came to class exercises, they both struggled because they prefer using their prior knowledge but they did not realize that the things had since changed or that the things were more complex than they thought.

In addition to being angry with me the learner had problems accessing the Internet! He was under the impression that I had blocked it. As much as I despise the practice, I do not ask them not to use the Internet during class. I know that other people can multi-task; others would doze if they were to fixate at me all day long. I am not that exciting!

The reason I am saying all this is that, some learners will just dislike you for simple reasons like a small misunderstanding. As a result and may be as expected, I got the worst reviews from both of them. The background information I have given is very important when reading the evaluations. Here is a situation. This particular class had 8 learners. I received largely perfect scores from the 6. Comments ranged from 'The best trainer ever', 'Other trainers should learn from him', to 'This is the training we should have had from the start', etc, then all of a sudden two bombshells. During the time they were writing the evaluation, one of them messed the form and asked for a fresh one. It was clear that there was something he wanted to change.

As fate would have it, their evaluations were the ones I read. . Also, seven of them wrote their names on the evaluation forms even though the form said the name was optional. This meant that I knew what everyone said even the one who did not put his name down. It was the individual that I misunderstood. How could their evaluation be seen as objective when the evaluation of the rest of the class was sharply different?

As you can see from the statements above, evaluations should be evaluated and put into perspective. Getting good remarks may mean that I was genuinely good or it may mean the learners are being nice to me just in case we happen to work together in future. The poor remarks could be the objective ones or could be a defense for their inability to cope with the class.

However an evaluation is a sharp knife that cuts both ways. In the words of Aretha Franklin and Narada Michael Walden, 'Who is zooming who? Are you zooming me or am I zooming you?' In this case, by reading these contrasting remarks, it could be that the learners evaluated themselves and have reflected their mentality, personality and their sentiments towards the trainer and the training. However, I am a professional. I asked for evaluations and that is what I got. They are therefore 'immune' from 'criticism'.

'End of the road' - My training closing remarks

You may have seen graduation ceremonies in many movies where the school principal, or the commander (if it is a military graduation) gives a 'sending off speech' to the graduating class. I usually use a diluted approach at the end of each day together with my summary of the events of the day.

On the last day, I say a bit more. I summarize the objectives of the course and highlight how far we met them. In addition I mention how that knowledge gained in the training meets the job needs. I talk on how they can improve their job by applying what was learnt. I sometimes point out what further training may be necessary to achieve a certain level in the careers. I also thank them for attending and participating in the class exercises.

Here is a sample of what I would say:

"Well, congratulations everyone for you have made it to the end of the training. It has been two weeks and I know that it has been long and at times bumpy but due to your commitment we made it. No matter how many times I give training, no two training sessions are ever the same. As much as you may think that you have learnt, I have learnt as much. The questions that you asked, the suggestions you made, and the knowledge that you shared, has not only enriched me with knowledge, but also made me look at the subject matter from a different perspective and therefore I have seen and learnt something new from a subject I thought I already knew well. It is true when they say 'One never stops to learn'. I am glad I was here and I hope it has been worthwhile for you too. Please bear in mind that the coverage of this training is not exhaustive. It has just pointed you in the right direction. For your career growth, you owe it to yourselves to continue seeking growth and improvement in the work that you do. Use this knowledge and identify its limits in order to identify any further training you may need. I am interested to know how you will be doing. You can always reach me by e-mail. I thank you for attending the class, your participation, and sharing your experiences that have contributed to the success of this training. I send you out with good wishes. I hope you do well. It is a small world and we might meet again. God Bless!"

Appendices

Appendix A - setup your laptop as a local server

Settings

The following steps describe how to setup your computer as a computer server for other computers to connect to it in order to execute an application on it.

1. Depending on the operation system you are using, navigate to 'Network Connections'. For Windows XP operating system, click Start Menu and point your mouse to 'Settings'.

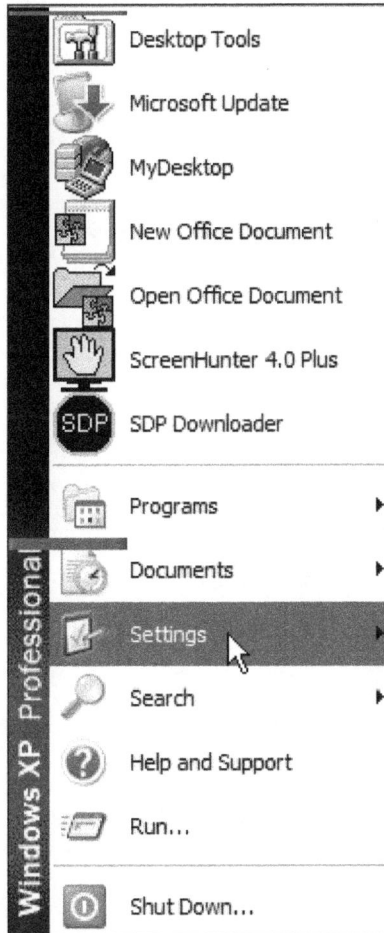

2. This sub-Menu displays:

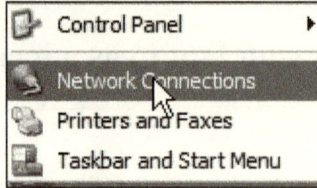

3. Click on 'Network Connections'.

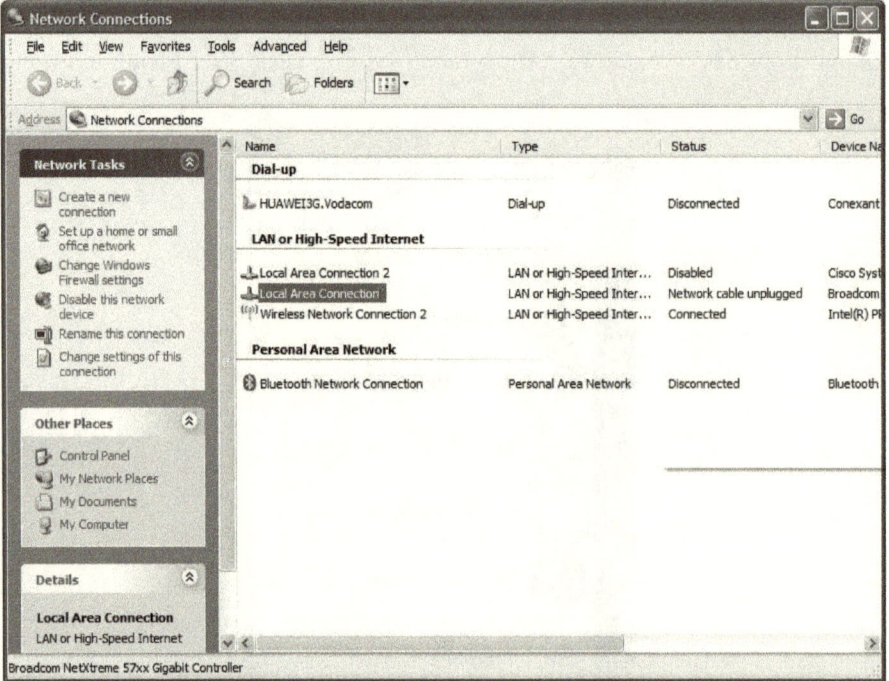

4. Right-click on the 'Local Area Connection'.

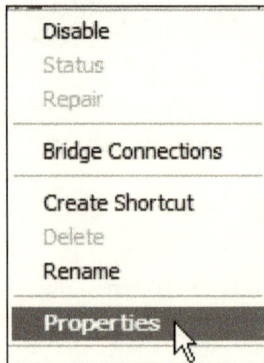

5. Click on 'Properties'.

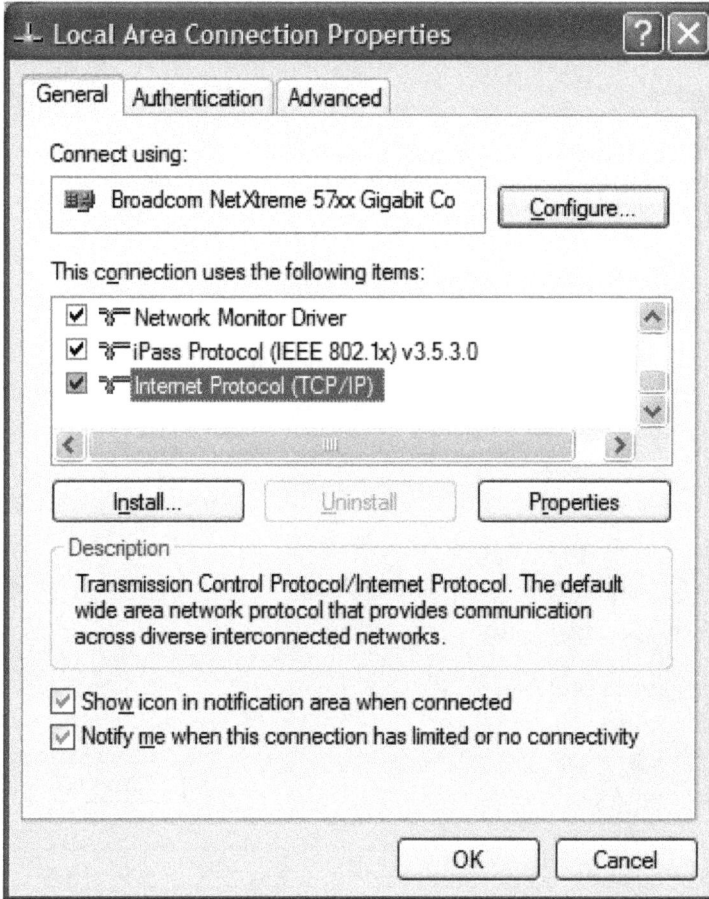

6. Scroll down in 'This connection uses the following items', click on 'Internet Protocol (TCP/IP), and click on 'Properties'.

Internet Protocol (TCP/IP) Properties

General

You can get IP settings assigned automatically if your network supports this capability. Otherwise, you need to ask your network administrator for the appropriate IP settings.

○ Obtain an IP address automatically

◉ Use the following IP address:

IP address: 192 . 168 . 0 . 1

Subnet mask: 255 . 255 . 255 . 0

Default gateway: . . .

○ Obtain DNS server address automatically

◉ Use the following DNS server addresses:

Preferred DNS server: . . .

Alternate DNS server: . . .

Advanced...

OK   Cancel

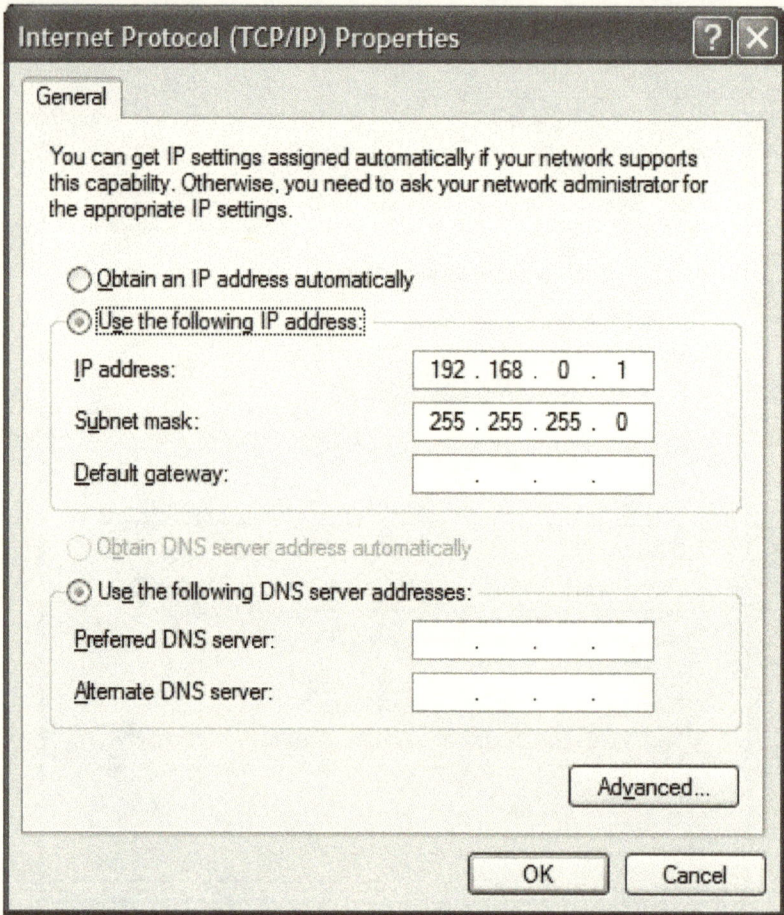

7. Click on 'Use the following IP address', enter 'IP address' and 'Subnet Mask' entered as an example, and click OK button.

Using the setup

On each terminal computer connected to the server via a computer hub, type 'http://192.168.0.1/applicationName' on the Internet Browser to execute the application.

Appendix B - setup extended monitor feature

Settings

The following steps describe how to setup your computer to switch on two monitors - one for the projector and the other for your computer.

1. Right-click on Desktop.

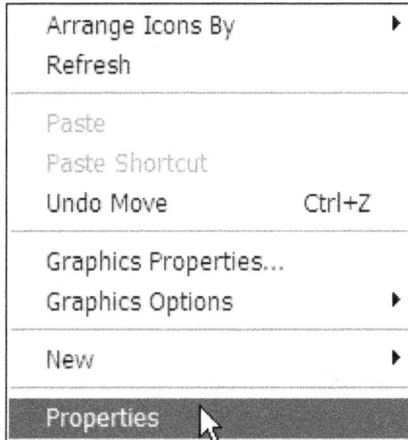

2. Click on Properties.

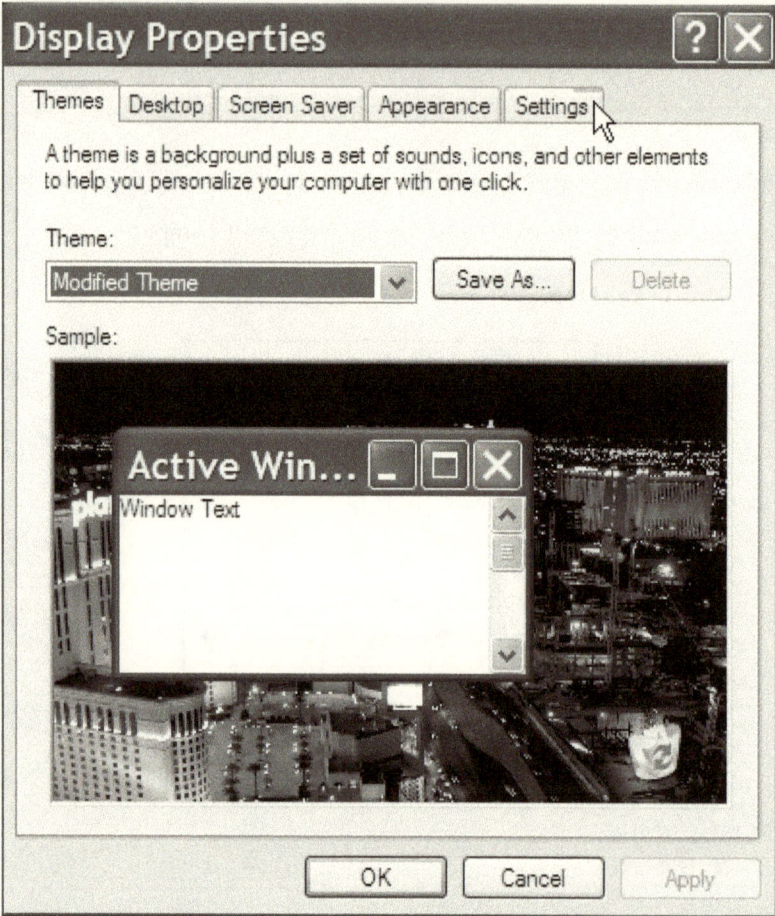

3. Click on Settings tab.

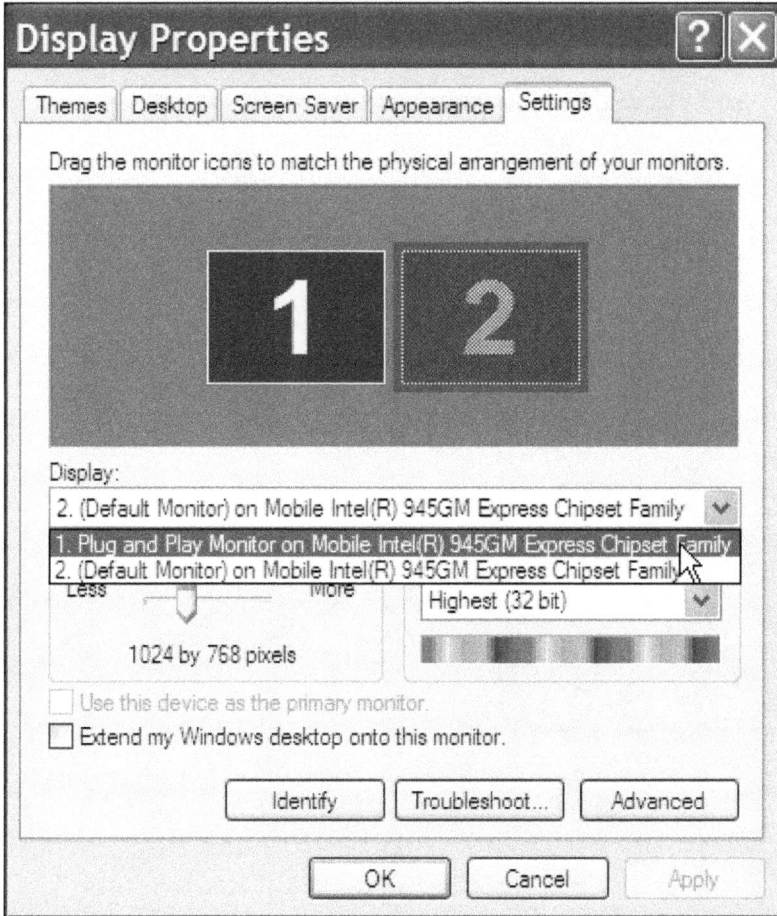

4. Click Display and select option 1.

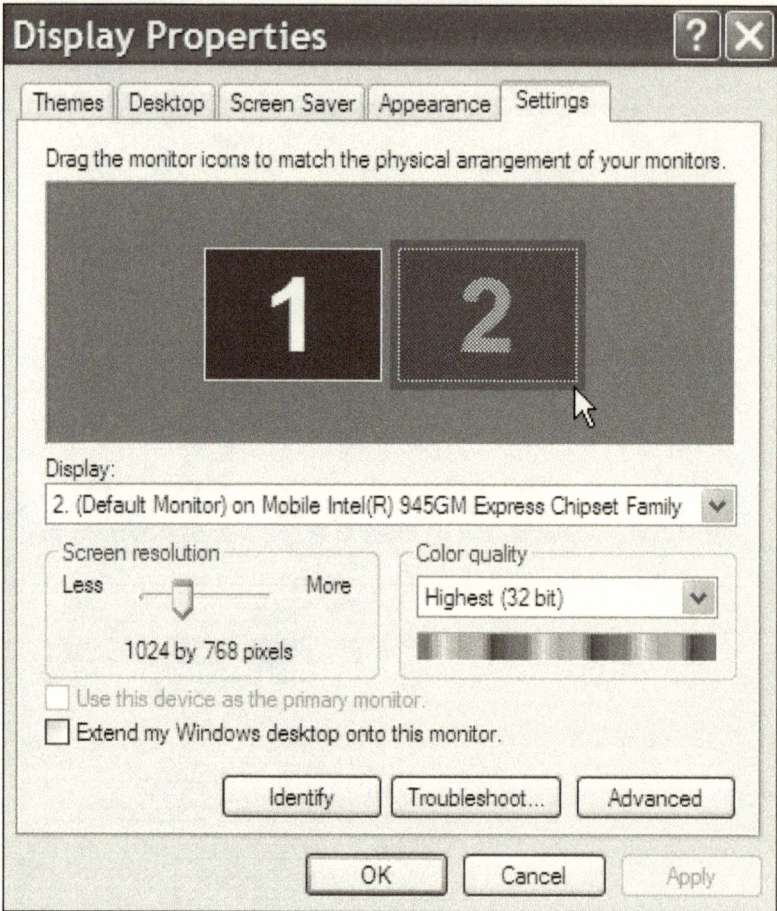

5. Click on Screen 2.

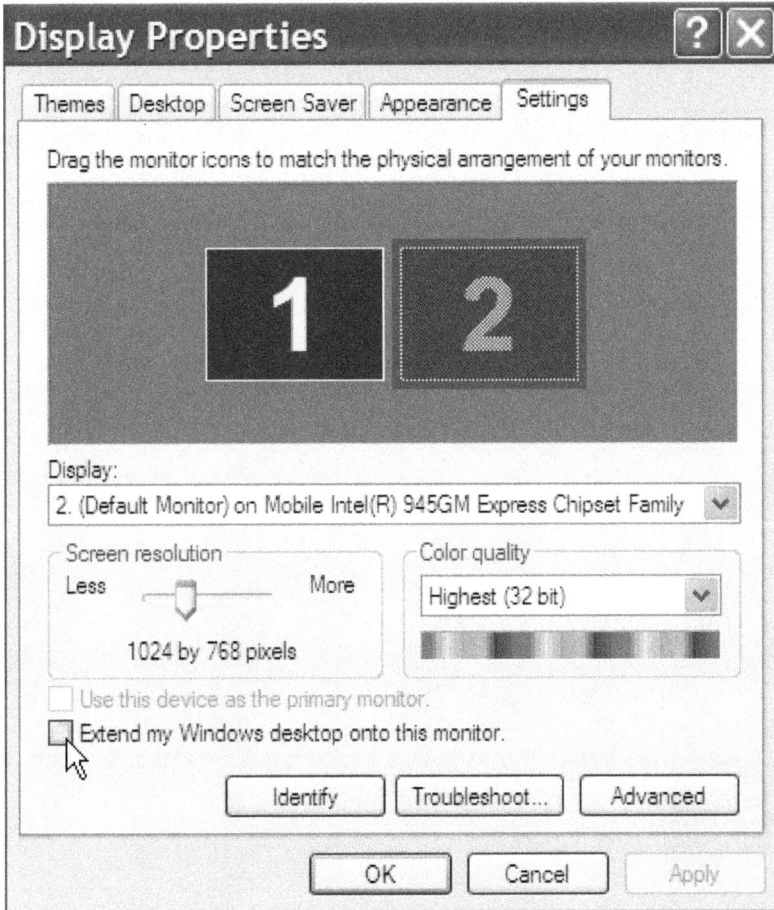

6. Click check box 'Extend my Window desktop onto this monitor.'

Using the setup

1. Reboot your computer to enable the feature to take effect.

2. Open your document.

3. Click Restore/Maximize icon of the document that you want to display on the projector in order to switch to Restore mode which enables you to drag it.

4. Drag this document off your computer screen and it will be displayed on the projector.

5. To remove it from the projector, move your mouse cursor to the projected document and drag it back to your computer screen.

www.ingramcontent.com/pod-product-compliance
Lightning Source LLC
Chambersburg PA
CBHW031959080426

42735CB00007B/448